Apisaloma & Fialelei,

May the Lord bring
daily increase in your love
for each other. Let HIM
rule at all times,

Phil 1:6

God bless and prosper
all that you do in Jesus
name.

Love & Peace

Len

The Road to Self-Worth
(A BOOK FOR DISCIPLES)

PART ONE
Marriage & Relationships

BY
LEO BOGEE JR.

Bloomington, IN   authorHOUSE   Milton Keynes, UK

AuthorHouse™
1663 Liberty Drive, Suite 200
Bloomington, IN 47403
www.authorhouse.com
Phone: 1-800-839-8640

AuthorHouse™ UK Ltd.
500 Avebury Boulevard
Central Milton Keynes, MK9 2BE
www.authorhouse.co.uk
Phone: 08001974150

This book is a work of non-fiction. Unless otherwise noted, the author and the publisher make no explicit guarantees as to the accuracy of the information contained in this book and in some cases, names of people and places have been altered to protect their privacy.

First published by AuthorHouse 01/25/06

ISBN: 1-4208-9632-6 (sc)

Printed in the United States of America
Bloomington, Indiana

This book is printed on acid-free paper.

***

*This book is dedicated first and foremost
to my wife, Christine. Thank you for pointing
me toward the <u>light</u> during my darkest night. You
are a woman of wisdom, honor, integrity, humility,
and character. I thank God for your love.
I love you.*

&

*This book is dedicated to my parents,
Leo J. Bogee, Sr. and Eunice I. Bogee.
Their fifty years of marriage is a prototype
for declaration, commitment, and
love in marriage and family.*

***

Table of Contents

PREFACE

I believe there are three areas of personal growth that impact our lives on a daily basis. They are relationships, leadership, and an awareness of who you are as a person. This book is written to address the first of these three areas, and that is the area of relationships. Relationships lay the foundation for the development of sound leadership and provide validation for who you are as a person. Without relationships there would be no one to lead; and it would be impossible to establish societies, churches, and organizations.

Of course, our ultimate relationship is with our Lord and Creator, God the Father. His designed purpose from the beginning was to have a personal relationship with each person He created. Adam and Eve had that kind of relationship. God also gave them "free will" and with their free will came the ability to choose between God and evil. They would soon find out that evil desires lead to sin. However, with the introduction of sin into their lives, things began to change rapidly. Sin brought separation between mankind and God. However, God already had a plan to restore mankind to their original place and role in His Creation.

God gave Eve to Adam to be his wife. Marriage was the first relationship created between two human beings. These two human beings were clearly a man and a woman. Marriage is therefore the most important relationship God gave to mankind, and marriage is the foundation for all relationships between a man and a woman. Since relationships are important to God, they are also important to the enemy of God. Godly relationships will always be under attack and marked for destruction.

Therefore, it is vitally important to know and to understand that mankind has an adversary and that adversary is the devil. The devil is Satan. He is the fallen archangel whose name was Lucifer. Satan is a single being and cannot be in more than one place at the same time. He doesn't have to be in more than one place at a time, because he has plenty of help from his cohorts, demonic spirits. Demonic spirits are assigned to principalities, powers, and the rulers of darkness that reside in certain areas of the world. They are assigned to do three things and three things only, and they are: to steal, to kill, and to destroy. As you will see in the first three chapters, these demonic spirits hate human beings. They hate those who have given their lives to Jesus and they especially hate those who have given their vows in a Christian marriage. The main weapon of their attack is deception. Of course, deception works best on those who don't know, understand, or believe that they are under attack by demonic forces. As long as you remain in denial of these demonic forces, you will blame other human beings for all your troubles. You will avoid relationships with people and miss God's call on your life.

Relationships are an integral part of God's plan for all of mankind. No one was created to be alone. During your time here on Earth, take advantage of the opportunities to be in relationship with as many people as possible. Each time that you do, you will grow and be strengthened in your walk with God. Actually, your relationship with other people defines your true relationship with God. You cannot love God and hate people. God has no Lone Ranger Christians. It is through relationships that God grows His Church.

On this *"Road to Self-Worth,"* be cognizant of God's most Holy Spirit. He will lead you into relationship after relationship in order to help you fulfill the assignment that He has on your life. Let each person see the Jesus that dwells in your heart. Be willing to receive feedback (their experience of you in words) from other people in order to reveal the things that you need to change in your life. God only reveals to heal, not to hurt or embarrass or condemn you. God commands you to transform and renew your mind. The only way to do that is to make changes in your heart. All successful relationships will require you to make changes in your heart.

I hope that this book will help you grasp the common-sense meaning of the Word of God for relationships and be able to apply it in your life. The time you have here on Earth is all you get. This is not practice, but reality. You have an assignment from God that only you can fulfill. It certainly involves other people. Prepare yourself to have successful relationships, and if you choose a gloriously successful marriage. Get ready to be blessed.

Don't take anything to the grave that God gave you to use and to share while you are here on the Earth.

Praise the Lord!

***

INTRODUCTION

The *"Road to Self-Worth"* is a three-part journey from the present into the future. Of course, you can look back in the past to see how things were, or how you acted in certain situations. If you do, I think you will find that the past is not as important as the secular world's teachings would have you believe. It is the present that defines your life and the future that drives your life. Yes, the past did happen, but there is nothing whatsoever you can do to change, fix, or alter it. Thank God for that.

Because you are a dimensional creation, you think in terms of past, present, and future. However, you only exist in the present. Your thought process, from information received from the past, prepares you to act on that information in the present, thereby creating a tangible future. The more time you spend aware of and focused on the present, the greater your accomplishments will be. That's why, in the eyes of God, the greatest accomplishment a person can achieve is to tell someone else about His Son, Jesus. Tell someone your testimony (from the past), so that they can take action in the present (accept Jesus), and create a future greater than anything they had dreamed possible. This is your role and the greatest assignment that you can complete before you die.

This book has taken about ten years to write. In July 1995, I began to write a book on leadership. I had just returned home from a church seminar. I had an uncanny urge to write. I began to write on a whiteboard, and within an hour, I had a twelve-chapter outline for my book on leadership. I began to write and finally completed a 300-page manuscript. It needed a lot more work, as I found out at a writers' workshop. I knew it would take a lot more time and focus before it would be ready for publishing.

Another question I had was how leadership was going to fit into the daily lives of most people. It did not seem to make sense for someone to only read about leadership when they were not in leadership. So, I just left the manuscript in a drawer for over four years. During this four-year period, I was exposed to numerous church leaders with every ministry you could think of. It was during this time that I began to be inspired to redirect my writing to coincide with what the Word of God had to say on church leadership. I believe

I was directed to write about leadership in the light of the culture of Christianity, as opposed to the secular view on leadership.

I spent twenty-five years on active duty in the military. I was one of the 1 percent of the U.S. Navy enlisted who attained the rank and position of Command Master Chief (CMC), the Senior Enlisted Advisor to the Commanding Officer. I had been to numerous leadership courses and I even taught some of them. I had developed a four-day leadership course (eight hours a day) that had literally changed the lives of many of those who attended. In one of the three Commands in which I served as the CMC, I experience the real impact of this leadership course. I had other CMC's asking about the training and could they have my "notes" on the training. I told them it wasn't just the notes, but the experience that made the changes. Of course, they would not attend and see for themselves.

What got their attention was a ten-month period in which there were no (I mean absolutely none) Captain's Masts (that is an Article 15 in other Armed Services) in my Command. (Captain's Masts and Articles 15's are non-judicial hearings for violations of military laws and standards. The Commanding Officers have the power to impose punishment or dismissal of the charges that have been brought against individuals accused of violating military laws. These Masts are often held weekly in many Commands.) To have a ten month period without any Masts was unheard of in my career. I knew I had something very special in that leadership course.

Many of those who took the leadership course seemed to have attained a higher personal level of responsibility, accountability, and self-worth. Their change spread throughout the Command and changed how we all related to each other and even more so to our patients/customers (this was a Medical Command). I saw similar results in my other Commands, as well as in the secular companies, organizations, and institutions in which I presented this leadership course.

When I introduced the leadership course into the church setting, the results were even more pronounced. This made me aware of the distinctions between leadership in the military and in the church. In the military, leadership is <u>fear-based</u>; do as I say and not as I do and do not ask questions. In the church, leadership is vision-based (or should be). It should support the vision that God has imparted into the pastor's heart for that particular congregation.

I guess you must be wondering, where is the book on leadership? It is coming soon to a bookstore near you. I believe I was directed to first publish this book on marriage and relationships. Because before you can lead you must have someone to lead. Leadership is based on relationships with people not isolation from people. Jesus built His church on relationships and marriage is the foundation for all relationships. Jesus is the Head of the church and the church is the bride of Jesus Christ. Jesus is the most powerful and effective leader who ever lived. And everything that He did, He did through relationships with people.

The "Road to Self-Worth" is a three-part journey, as I said earlier. Part One is *Marriage and Relationships*; Part Two is *Leadership*; and Part Three is *Personal Awareness.* I believe that once the foundation for marriage and relationships has been established, then the leaders will come forth with the power needed to complete their calling. The perception of who you are is based on your self-worth. You can only become a leader when you believe it yourself. If you do not know who you are, then how can you receive commands from God? God chose Gideon and David because He saw who they were, long before they could see their greatness. Once they understood who they were, they began to act differently and act boldly, in order to accomplish what the Lord called them to do.

As I explore relationships, in particular marriage, based on what the Bible says about them, be ready to check out any and all claims that I make concerning the Bible text. I will be quoting from the New King James (NKJ) version for the most part, but I will let you know when I quote any other version.

Let me be clear about my beliefs concerning the use of the Bible as my source and foundation for this book on marriage and relationships. I believe that the Bible is the Word of God and the Bible is truth. I promise to do my best with the guidance of the Holy Spirit to present what I believe to be God's Word on the subject of marriage and relationships. I have coached/counseled/trained hundreds of couples and thousands of individuals over the past twenty-six years. The answer, the solution to every one of their problems was and is the Word of God. It is the application of the Word of God that heals, restores, and strengthens marriages and relationships, and nothing else.

This book was written primarily to and for those who have chosen to be Disciples of the Lord Jesus Christ. It is also written to believers in hope of their transformation into disciples. There is a difference. A disciple will be there when you need them and be there doing their part every Sunday morning. A believer will be there based on how they feel or if their favorite team is not playing that Sunday at the time of the service. All believers should have a desire to become disciples. Christians do not mature with time necessarily, but they do mature by their pursuit of the Word of God. Disciples are in hot pursuit of God's best for their lives through their service to Him.

This book is also written to nonbelievers who are seeking answers for their life's problems. This book is not the answer, but Jesus is the answer. I pray that this book will lead them to the Lord and inspire them to read the Bible for themselves to see firsthand what God has prepared for those who believe in His Son, Jesus.

The End Times are here. The Body of Christ needs everyone doing their part. The Body of Christ must come together in unity and in faith. There is still much work to be done, and therefore, every worker must do his or her part. Who are you in Christ? What has Jesus called you to do in your lifetime? Are you willing to do it?

The Gospel will be preached throughout the whole world, the Bible tells us so. The question still remains, how will you do your part to prepare this planet for the return of Jesus? If you want to know what your part is, then read on. I pray that the Lord will surely reveal in your heart everything that He has for you to accomplish. His anointing will accompany His gifts to ensure your great success. I pray that you will be blessed for the seed that you have sown into this ministry by the purchase of this book.

To God be all the glory!

***

Prayer of Salvation

Of course, if you have not received Jesus as your Lord and Savior, then that is the first step. Give your life over to the Lord Jesus. Open up your heart to receive all the promises of God and all the blessings of God. Receive your salvation and a place with the Lord Jesus for all eternity. Just read the following passage and confess out loud the prayer that follows:

"If you confess with your mouth the Lord Jesus and believe in your heart that God has raised Him from the dead, you will be saved. 10 For with the heart one believes unto righteousness, and with the mouth confession is made unto salvation."
(Romans 10:9-10)

Prayer of salvation: (pray out loud)

**Father God, I come before you in the name of Jesus.
I believe in my heart that Jesus died for my sins.
I believe You raised Jesus from the dead and He
is alive and in heaven. I confess that
Jesus is now my Lord and Savior. I repent of all my
sin. I renounce Satan and all his evil works. I believe
that I am saved and one day I will be with You in
heaven for all eternity. I believe that I am now
a born-again follower of Jesus Christ.
I praise you, Lord!
amen**

If you prayed this prayer, you are now born-again. All your sins are forgiven, every sin from the first time you (knowingly) sinned until this moment. You are now a Christian.

Praise the Lord!

- If you do not have a Bible, get one and read it
daily. Start with the New Testament and read
as much as you can daily.
- If you do not belong to a Christian church,
then find one in your area, or e-mail me and
I will help you locate a believing church.
- God has great things ahead for you, so get
into fellowship with other believers and disciples
who can help you, teach you, and edify you.

Congratulations!

Welcome to the Body of Christ.

***

CHAPTER ONE
IN THE
BEGINNING

**"He created them male and female, and blessed
them and called them Mankind (Adam/
man) in the day they were created."
(Genesis 5:2)**

In the beginning, God created the heavens and the Earth, the night and the day, the sky and the water, the mountains and the valleys, the oceans and the rivers, the birds and the insects, the animals and the fish. God also made mankind, both the male and the female and called them both Adam/man, and God said that it was good. God also created the angels, and like mankind, He gave them free will.

Of all the angels and powerful archangels, one was willing to corrupt himself and fall from the presence of God. The archangel's name was Lucifer and he was cast down to the Earth (and Jesus said "**I saw Satan fall like lightning from heaven**" (Luke 10:18)) and he then became known as Satan. Along with him fell one-third of the host of angels and they would never return to heaven. (**⁴"His tail drew a third of the stars of heaven and threw them to the Earth..."** ⁹**"Therefore rejoice, O heavens, and you who dwell in them! Woe to the inhabitants of the Earth and the sea for the devil has come down to you, having great wrath, because he knows that he has a short time**" (Revelation 12:4 and 12:9).

God created everything and said that it was good. However, He did not say that everything that His creations did was good. He knew that by creating free will, something other than good would be possible. Free will demands that a choice is available. The ultimate free will, choice, is the same today as it was then. That choice was and is between God and evil. All creatures with free will must make that choice. Satan chose evil through the sin of pride.

Adam and Eve chose the sin of disobedience. It did not matter so much which sin they chose, because all sin leads to death of the body and spirit (James 1:15): **"Then, when desire has conceived, it gives birth to sin; and sin, when it is full-grown, brings forth death."** However, it did matter that they chose evil and not God. It also shows the consequences of the choices that they made and the permanence of those consequences.

Satan's sin of pride brought forth the consequences of death and the creation of "the lake of fire and brimstone" (Revelation 20:10): **"The devil, who deceived them, was cast into the lake of fire and brimstone where the beast and the false prophet are. And they will be tormented day and night forever and ever."** It is a decision (indecision is a decision) by all beings created with a free will that determines where they will spend all of eternity. The choice of God over evil is the ultimate decision. Every creature that was created with free will must make that choice.

The choice of Jesus Christ as your Lord and Savior over Satan as your lord and destroyer is the final decision that will determine where you will spend eternity. God is just. He fully expects mankind to reject evil and choose Jesus. His Word says in Romans 10:9-13, **⁹"that if you <u>confess with your mouth the Lord Jesus</u> and <u>believe in your heart that God has raised Him from the dead, you will be saved.</u> ¹⁰For with the heart one believes unto righteousness and with the mouth confession is made unto salvation. ¹¹For the Scripture says, whoever believes on Him will not be put to shame. ¹²For there is no distinction between Jew and Greek, for the same Lord over all is rich to all who call upon Him. ¹³For whoever calls on the name of the LORD shall be saved. Also, in John 14:6, "Jesus said to him, I am the way, the truth, and the life. No one comes to the Father except through Me."**

Satan was the first to choose evil over God. His punishment is to spend all eternity in the lake of fire and brimstone (Revelation 20). The lake of fire and brimstone was never intended for mankind. It requires a conscious choice of evil over God to be thrown into the lake of fire and brimstone (Revelation 20:15); **¹⁵"And anyone not found written in the Book of Life was cast into the lake of fire."** It is clearly stated in the Book of Romans 12:9; **"if you confess with your mouth the Lord Jesus and believe in your heart that God raised Him from the dead, you will be saved."** The choice is up to each individual person.

As I stated before, indecision is a decision, therefore, not making a decision to believe in Jesus is choosing evil over God. There is no fence to stand on with the Lord. There is no gray area with the Lord.

3

You are a creation with free will and you will be held accountable for everything that you do, say, and believe in your heart. This life you live is not a dress rehearsal, but the only life you'll have before dying. God will not make anyone choose His Son, Jesus, by overriding their free will.

Satan knows his fate and he only wants to steal, kill, and destroy everything that mankind has. (John 10:10): **"The thief does not come except to steal, and to kill, and to destroy. I have come that they may have life, and that they may have it more abundantly."** He has a plan for the total destruction of mankind, but he does not have the power to carry it out. He needs the help of each individual person. He needs your permission and cooperation. Every plan against humanity that he has tried to implement has failed. However, he has duped many people in the process. He knows he cannot win and will not win, so his hatred for humanity is great. The devil will not stop trying to steal, kill, and destroy until the final day of his miserable life.

Humanity is caught up in the devil's spiritual warfare battle and there is no way for mankind to win the battle without the Lord Jesus Christ, (I John 3:8): **"He who sins is of the devil, for the devil has sinned from the beginning. For this purpose the Son of God was manifested, that He might destroy the works of the devil."** You must be prepared for spiritual warfare at all times. The devil has many tricks and traps. The more you know about your enemy, the better prepared you will be to defeat him when his attacks come. You can only lose if you do not call on the name of Jesus.

The Plan

What would you do if you knew that someone, who was yet to be born, would one day come and destroy you and your entire family? What would your first reaction be? If you felt there was enough time, you would probably try to find out when and where this person would be born and do everything in your power to destroy him before he could be born. However, if there was no way possible to find out their birth date or the place, then you would probably try to destroy his mother, so that he would never be born (like in the movie *The*

Terminator). However, when you found out that you could not destroy his mother, then what would you do next?

This is not a make-believe scenario, but an example of what actually took place, some six thousand-plus years ago. A prophesy was given to the serpent (the devil, Satan himself), in the Garden of Eden. This prophesy was given to Satan, by God, in the form of punishment for deceiving Eve (Genesis 3:15): **"And I will put enmity between you and the woman, and between your seed and her Seed; He shall bruise your head, and you shall bruise His heel."**

The actual prophesy meant that the "Seed" of the woman would crush his head (destroy him and his kind). With this punishment, he knew that his plan to destroy mankind had already begun to backfire. His first reaction, as in the scenario above, was to kill the woman (Eve) outright; however, he found out he could not harm her physically. (You can see in the Book of Job that the devil cannot lay a hand on you without your permission.) (Job 1:12): **"And the LORD said to Satan, Behold, all that he has is in your power; only do not lay a hand on his person."** Therefore, the devil needed to devise a different plan of attack.

Of course, the simplest solution was to kill the human occupants of this exquisite planet call Earth. The devil had free reign above, on, and beneath the Earth until the Creator (God the Father Himself) place a man on the scene. God had given the man and the woman dominion over all the Earth. This infuriated the devil. It was in his attempt to regain control of the Earth that he decided to deceive the woman and bring about the downfall of mankind and put an end to the dominion of this God-like creature.

Since the devil didn't have the authority to physically harm the man or the woman, he had to find a way to get them to destroy themselves. He was nearby when he overheard the Creator tell the man not to eat the "fruit" of the Tree of the Knowledge of Good and Evil, or even touch it. He heard the Lord say, if he did he would surely die. He remembered those words and realized that he did not have to touch them at all. All he had to do is to get them to disobey the Creator and then sit back and watch them die.

5

Satan knew how much it bothered the humans to walk by the forbidden tree and not be able to touch it, let alone eat of its fruit. They had everything they could possibly want, and yet their desire was for the one thing they could not have. The tree became the focus of their "free will" choice. Satan believed their "free will" would be their downfall. He had exercised his right of free will and it had cost him his exalted position in heaven. He was no longer Lucifer, the beautiful angel of light, but Satan, prince of darkness. His sin of pride had caused his fall from heaven and transformed him into a creature of evil and the most hideous creature alive. He knew all too well the cost that free will could exact when exercised in disobedience to the Creator. He also understood that free will comes with only two choices: to choose God or to choose evil. He hoped with some certainty—since they were only humans—that mankind would choose evil as he had done. He also knew that disobedience was evil and all evil is sin; and the consequence of sin is death.

Satan began to implement his plan to entice mankind to disobey, to exercise their free will in direct defiance to the Word of the Creator. He knew it was only a matter of time before his temptation, his invitation to do evil, would be accepted. On that fateful day, when both the man and the woman ate of the fruit of the Tree of the Knowledge of Good and Evil, he rejoiced. The devil and all of his cohorts danced in celebration of the fall of the Creator's most prized creation, mankind. He believed he once again had dominion over things of the Earth and his darkness would reign once again. He would not have to fear the coming of the "Seed" of the woman, because there wouldn't be anyone alive to produce Him. The father of lies, the prince of darkness, and the lord of the flies thought he was in control again. However, the Creator had a different plan.

Although mankind had disobeyed and would have to suffer the consequences for their sins, the devil also was facing certain consequences for his sin of lying. He soon found out that the same thing that makes you laugh can also make you cry, especially when sin is involved. He watched as Adam and Eve ate the fruit. He watched and waited, but they did not die. He knew he had heard God and that it was impossible for God to lie, so why didn't they drop over dead?

He knew he would be subject to mankind once again when the "Seed" of the woman arrived. He was devastated. He asked himself over and over again, why didn't they die?

Adam and Eve did die. They died the same way Satan had died. They suffered spiritual death. Their physical death would come eventually, but not before their offspring covered the Earth. Now, Satan knew he would have to come up with a new plan and soon. This time he could not afford to fail. His very existence depended on the success of his next attempt to destroy mankind.

Since these humans were now on to him, he would have to be extra careful not to be exposed before he had certain victory in sight. The devil knew that Adam and Eve were not as protected as before. The Creator had removed his "anointed power" from around them. They had to work hard for everything they got. They were subject to sickness, disease, and bodily harm. Their eternal bodies were now dying and would once again be returned to the dust of the Earth, as God had promised them. However, the devil did not want to wait. No, he had to act now toward the complete destruction of mankind.

Soon after Adam and Eve were put out of the Garden of Eden, Eve conceived and gave birth to a son and named him Cain. After a little while, she conceived again and gave birth to another son and named him Abel. Satan was frantic. He watched as Eve bore two sons and waited in fear to see if either one on them was the "Seed" that was born to crush his head. Since he wasn't sure about which son it could be, he decided not to take any more chances. He began to implement a new plan that, if it worked, he could eliminate both sons. He unveiled his new plan and introduced a new weapon of his spiritual warfare into the family of Adam; he called it ANGER. He unleashed his attack on the older son. He knew from his own experience with anger that envy and jealousy would accompany it. Satan began to work on Cain's heart until everything his younger brother did offended him. At the right moment, when Cain's anger reached his desired measure, he would unleash another one of his powerful weapons for the final victory, and that was the sin of MURDER.

God knew what the devil was up to and He warned Cain about his anger. He told him that sin was very near to him (Genesis 4:6-7):

*⁶"So the L*ORD *said to Cain, 'Why are you angry? And why has your countenance fallen'? ⁷If you do well, will you not be accepted? And if you do not do well, sin lies at the door. And its desire is for you, <u>but you should rule over it.</u>"* Cain did not heed the Word of the Lord and murdered his brother, Abel.

I know you have probably been taught that Cain killed Abel because his offering offended God. His offering was from the field or garden and Abel's offering was sheep or meat. Maybe you thought that God only accepted meat and not produce for an offering. The substance of the offering had nothing to do with God's rejection of the offering. God did accept produce offerings; Cain knew it and that is why Cain offered it. He knew what God's rules were for offerings because he was the older brother and his father had taught him how to honor God. It had nothing to do with the offering being produce or meat, but it did have to do with the condition of his heart. Cain brought his offering while he was angry and contemplating murder and that is why God could not accept his offering. God even warned him, but Cain had already decided to choose evil over God. Cain refused to listen to God and led his brother into the fields and murdered him. Immediately, death was assigned to him.

God banished Cain from the presence of his parents and their land. Cain would have his own offspring and the iniquity in his heart would be passed down to their generation. Five generations later, another son would be born in Cain's lineage, by the name of Lamech, and he would murder another man. Sin and death had established firm footholds in the lives of mankind on the Earth. It seemed that Satan's plan was actually working, maybe not at the level he had expected, but it was working.

(The Bible says, *"Jesus (God) is the same yesterday, today, and forever"* (Hebrews 13:8). God accepts and rejects offerings today the same way He did 6,000 years ago. In the Gospel of Matthew 5:23-24, it says, *²³"Therefore, if you bring your gift to the altar, and there remember that your brother has something against you, ²⁴leave your gift there before the altar, and go your way. First be reconciled to your brother, and then come and offer your gift."* It will always be about the condition of your heart. The seed is often the same, but

8

the ground you sow into and condition of your heart will determine the return on your sowing. If you have been wondering why you haven't received a return on your sowing, check your heart, and see if that is the problem. Forgive or ask to be forgiven, then return to the altar and make your offering. Forgiveness is not a suggestion, but it is a command from God.)

Satan was again overjoyed. Just think about it. There were only four humans, and he had gotten rid of one without lifting a hand. Now, if only he could get Cain to kill Eve, his problems would be over. Without the woman, there would be no possibility of another offspring. However, Eve did conceive again and gave birth to another son and named him Seth (appointed). She gave birth to more sons and daughters, and the Earth was beginning to fill. Satan knew now that the "Seed" of the woman did not mean just Eve, but it could be any woman.

Once again, his plan was failing and he was constantly worried about the birth of the "Seed." Originally, he only had to worry about Eve and her sons, but now he had to worry about her daughters and all of the sons they would have. He knew it was only a matter of time before his destroyer would arrive. However, he believed he was beginning to better understand human beings, and the next time, he would put together a plan that would not fail.

Satan began to ponder day and night for an answer. What could he do? He could not physically destroy them, but he could deceive them. He also knew that they were made in the image and likeness of God, the Creator Himself, so they were really spirits living in Earth suits or as they liked to call them, human bodies. He began to focus on their spiritual nature and wondered where their weakness could be found. He continued to worry day and night about that fateful day when "Seed" of the woman would show up and crush him. He had to act fast and decisively.

The "Seed"

The devil began to wonder about the nature of this "Seed" of the woman. Where would this "Seed" come from? First of all, only the man had seed, not the woman. Why then did the Creator say the "Seed" of the woman? In order to crush his head, this "Seed" would have to be more powerful than any one of these human creatures. Actually, he began to think, this "Seed" would have to come from the Creator, God Himself. The woman would only be the receptacle by which this "Seed" would enter the world. He believed this had to be so, in order for God to fulfill his prophecy in the Garden of Eden. Now, he began to understand the nature of his task. His next move would be to ensure that the only seed that the woman would ever receive would be contaminated by evil. He had to find a way to supply all of the seed for mankind. He knew that his seed of evil would never produce anyone with the power to destroy him because it would have his nature. Therefore, he could not afford to leave any woman out of his plan.

The devil began to release a multitude of sins, which included the spirits of pride, jealousy, envy, hatred, and many other forms of evil. He commanded his forces to continually tempt and test mankind. However, even with this level of spiritual warfare, one man was able to overcome even this plan. The man's name was Enoch and he was the seventh generation of Adam. He refused to live his life in sin, and turned his heart toward God. I believed that Enoch did something that no other man had done before. Enoch repented to the Lord for his sins. Somehow, he knew that his Creator would forgive him and turn away His wrath. Enoch had faith in the God of his fathers. His faith so pleased God that God took him from the Earth without dying.

The Bible says that Enoch walked with God, (Genesis 5:24): *"And Enoch walked with God; and he was not, for God took him."* (Only one other person would be taken from the Earth into heaven by God without dying. That other person was the prophet Elijah (II Kings 2:11): *"and suddenly a chariot of fire appeared with horses of fire, and separated the two of them; and Elijah went up by a whirlwind into heaven."* The devil could not afford to have another Enoch.

10

The devil was infuriated after the failure with Enoch. This time he decided to go all out and make sure that no living human being would be left out. He knew that mankind was becoming more and more sinful, but God still was not moved to destroy them all. He knew that he wasn't far from his goal, but he had to move fast before something else went wrong. He finally got it! He finally knew how to get rid of these human creatures. He had the answer with him all along. Instead of using his evil friends (fallen angels) to just tempt mankind, he would use them to produce offspring. How perfect! The offspring from a union of sinful humans and fallen angels would certainly incur the "wrath of God" and rid the Earth of all human existence. He believed there was no way for the promised "Seed" to come from such evil. Satan knew he would finally win.

Satan immediately began to implement his plan. He began to gather all of the fallen angels that were rebellious enough to leave their assigned places in the heavens and on the Earth. Mankind was in awe of them and even called them "the sons of God." As they began to marry the daughters of man and produce offspring, mankind began to change, and many of their offspring grew to be giants. His plan was working better than he expected; every human being born from that day forward was contaminated with his seed of evil. The "Seed" promised more than a thousand years ago was never going to come.

The devil remembered what he heard God say to the woman, *"that her desire would be for her husband and he shall rule over you"* (Genesis 3:16). This was part of Eve's punishment for her sin.

Eve was created specifically to be a helpmate to her husband. But what did Adam need help doing? He had everything he needed or desired, so why was a helpmate needed? Adam needed help in one area of his life and that was in his praise and worship of the Lord.

Eve was Adam's equal in the eyes of God before they sinned. Her desire was for God from the beginning and He ruled over her. Now all of that had changed. The devil could see that woman's desire was now for her husband and for the creatures that were being produced. They would certainly rule over her too. These creatures were filling the Earth and evil reigned everywhere mankind was found. There was

11

no way that God would send the "Seed" to one of these evil creatures. This time the devil's plan was going to be a complete success.

Fact or Fiction

I know this may sound far-fetched, but the Bible states that it happened exactly that way. There are those who say that the devil and his fallen angels were spirits and therefore, could not have sexual relations with a human and produce a child. The Bible also says that each species reproduces after itself. It is true that the devil and the fallen angels are spirits; however, so are human beings. You are made in the image and likeness of God Himself. You are a spirit and you live in a body, or as the Apostle Paul called it, a tent. The true nature of mankind is spirit. One day, this tent will die, but the spirit that we really are will never die, and it will live for all eternity in either heaven or hell.

Genesis 1:25: ***"And God made the beast of the Earth according to its kind, cattle according to its kind, and everything that creeps on the Earth according to its kind, And God saw that it was good. Then God said Let Us (Trinity/Father-Son-Holy Spirit) make man in Our image, according to Our likeness..."*** God is a spirit and mankind is made in His image. Satan knew that spirits could produce spirits. Angels cannot produce humans and humans cannot produce angels, but together they can produce another type of creature called a demon. Although they were produced in the Old Testament, they are not mentioned until the New Testament.

Where did all of these "sons of God" come from? They fell with Satan from heaven. When he fell, a third of the angels fell with him. He was not the only evil creature on the Earth and in the atmosphere. These fallen angels were given their assignments in this new environment and he knew where to find them. (Ephesians 6:12): ***"For we do not wrestle against flesh and blood, but against principalities, against powers, against the rulers of the darkness of this age, against spiritual hosts of wickedness in the heavenly places."*** These fallen angels, or spirits of evil, were already in place and ready to work in concert with the prince of evil to destroy mankind. The devil had to believe he would be completely successful in this all-out attempt to destroy mankind and maintain his dominion over the Earth. He must have been delighted in himself. This plan would guarantee the "Seed" of the woman would never be born; and his power and earthly kingdom would be restored forever.

Once again, there was a small detail the devil left out and without control of that one detail, his plan was destined for complete and utter failure. He failed to recognize that he could no more control the "free will" of mankind than God could. God gave mankind free will so that they could make choices as individuals and be totally responsible for their choices. He would never interfere with any of His creation's free will choices. However, the devil thought he could manipulate mankind to the point of their total submission to his authority. He would find out the hard way that mankind was truly made in the image and likeness of God. With free will, mankind was and is as unpredictable as the devil is predictable.

I am sure without a second thought, the devil launched his plan. To God goes the glory, for mankind is *"fearfully and wonderfully made"* (Psalms 139:14). Just as the devil began his attack, God launched His next plan toward the full salvation and restoration of humanity.

Every plan of the devil will meet with certain defeat. It is up to each person to read and understand the Word of God. It is only through the Word that the devil can be defeated. Far too many Christians live in fear of the devil because they do not know who they are in Christ Jesus. It is imperative that every Christian read their Bible. The power is there and all of the answers are there in the Word of God.

The road to self-worth leads directly to the throne room of the Lord God. Stay focused on the Word. Take authority over fear. Be bold and courageous as a man or woman of God. The devil is already defeated, so do not give him back any power that the Lord has already taken away from him.

Remember, the battle is the Lord's. God will be there to fight every battle for you. The victory is yours. Stand still and see the glory of the Lord for your life. God's plan for your life is always for good.

Praise the Lord!

***

CHAPTER TWO
GOD'S PLAN

"Then He will also say to those on the left hand, 'Depart from Me, you cursed, into the everlasting fire prepared for the devil and his angels'..."
(Matthew 26:41)

About 2,000 years after Satan began to implement his evil plan for mankind, God the Almighty, the Creator of heaven and Earth began to implement **phase two** of His plan for mankind. Did I mention **phase one** of God's plan? It was the plan to create mankind with a **free will.** This gift of a free will would distinguish mankind from all other creatures alive on the Earth. Free will gave mankind the unique ability to choose between God and evil, not good and evil, but God and evil.

In order for there to be free will, there must be something to choose. I have heard people teach that angels do not have free will. If that is true, then how did one-third of them fall along with Lucifer? Since they were created to worship God, nothing could have changed that if they did not have a free will. However, if they did have a free will, then choosing not to worship God was a possible. Angels did have a choice and they did have free will. They chose to sin, and spiritual death was the result. They are separated from the Lord and Creator for all eternity by their own choice. That is why God created hell, for the fallen angels. They freely rejected the glory and majesty of the presence of God in heaven. Now they will spend eternity without the glory and majesty of God Almighty. Hell is the antithesis of heaven.

The free will object or focus for mankind, represented by Adam, was the Tree of the Knowledge of Good and Evil. Adam knew what his choice to serve God was all about, but he did not know what his life would be like if he did not. He knew that it would bring death, because God had told him. He had to understand what death meant, or it would not have been a deterrent. However, since he had not seen another human being actually die, then that "room for doubt" did exist and the devil exploited that doubt. It wasn't because of Eve that Adam sinned, but because of his own free will choice that he sinned. That is why God punished Adam, Eve, and the devil individually.

Sin is always an individual act, but iniquity (evil or wickedness) is a lifestyle and it can be passed down from generation to generation. By choosing a lifestyle of evil, mankind also chose hell or the lake of fire that burns for all eternity.

Of course, anytime we choose against the commands of God, it involves sin. Adam's choice of the forbidden fruit involved idolatry, lust, pride, and disobedience, to name a few. That's why I said it is a choice of God or evil, not just good and bad. Our free will choices are either righteous or sinful, where God's commands are concerned. Sin also requires an understanding of what you are doing. Adam chose to sin, and knew it involved death. We must know that it is sinful before it is accounted as sin. That is why children cannot sin until they reach the age of reason, or the age of understanding God from evil.

I have heard many people say that they were saved when they were children, some as early as four years old. You can certainly say you accepted Jesus at any age, but you cannot know the difference between Jesus and evil at such an early age. You must have reached the age of reason in order to sin. For most people, it is around twelve years of age, but it can be earlier or later. Therefore, if you have never sinned, then you are already saved and will go to heaven if you die. Only after you have sinned is salvation through Christ Jesus required.

Salvation is the way into heaven for the sinner, and the Bible says that *"all mankind is sinful"* in Romans 3:23. However, sin is not possible for a child, and therefore, salvation is not needed for a child. Children do go to heaven when they die. Their free will is not in place, because they are not mature enough to choose between God and evil until later in life. This is very important that parents get this point. The role of Christian parents is to teach their children right from wrong during their training years, approximately one and a half to five years of age. I hope it brings comfort to parents who have lost their children at an early age to know, without any doubt, that they are with the Lord in heaven.

God taught mankind right from wrong in the days of Moses, by giving him and the Israelites the Ten Commandments. The Ten Commandments were given to expose what sin was. "Thou shalt not" does not mean that "thou shalt not be able to do." God was training them up in the way they should go and with the training, He attached consequences: ***"Foolishness is bound up in the heart of a child, the rod of correction will drive it far from him"*** (Proverbs 22:15). This rod of correction is discipline, not punishment. Discipline brings correction to the direction or path that a person is heading. It is an adjustment in behavior that will make a permanent change in and for the future.

Additionally, God corrects or disciplined those He loves: ***"My son, do not despise the chastening of the LORD, nor detest His correction; For whom the LORD loves He corrects, just as a father the son in whom he delights"*** (Proverbs 3:11-12). If the child will receive the discipline, then punishment will not be necessary in the future. If Christian parents will discipline their children, then the world will not have to punish them in the future. A good example is the terrible twos. The terrible twos are an invention of the world system. The rod of correction will drive it (the terrible part) out. If parents don't drive it out in the terrible twos, then they will have to deal with rebellion in the terrible teens. From age two to thirteen is eleven years, and that is a long time for rebellion to develop in a child. If you won't deal with your two-year-old, then your thirteen-to-eighteen-year-old will deal with you. Remember, we are talking about free will, and free will must be given direction, discipline, and focus in order for godly choices to be made.

Let me add this note at no additional charge. When a child (who has not reached the age of reason) takes a cookie after you told him not to take it, did he sin? When a child does not tell you the truth when you ask him about something he did, did he tell a lie, and therefore sin? Since you are born without sin (with the death and resurrection of Jesus Christ) and a child has not reached the age of reason, then how can he or she sin? Children are not thieves or liars; they are in their training phase. They are in their behavior adjustment phase and they need discipline, correction, and direction from people who love them—their parents and their church family.

Proverbs 22:6 says, ***"Train up a child in the way he should go and when he is old he will not depart from it."*** Childhood is a training period. Children must learn about God as well as sin and evil. Teach them right from wrong and begin to prepare them so that they will understand good from bad, and finally God from evil. If you are a parent, then training up your child so that he or she will better understand the choices they make, the consequences of those choices, and just how their free will works.

Additionally, if you have children who do not tell you the truth, then you need to focus on the reason. Why does anyone lie instead of telling the truth? Lying is fear-based. When people are afraid, they will use any means possible to save themselves from the thing they fear, even if the thing they fear is not real. (Fear is in the future because it does not exist. It is **F**alse **E**vidence **A**ppearing **R**eal. Fear is made up in the present because of something that happened in the past. Fear is the anticipation of something being repeated from a past <u>experience</u>.) If you are a parent and your children fear you, then expect them to lie to you. <u>The real issue is not about them lying, but about what kind of parent are you being that your children cannot or will not tell you the truth</u>. When you become a parent that they can tell the truth to, then they will stop lying to you.

(The above is true for anyone who is wondering why people seem to lie to them. The person is responsible for their lies, but the real issue is who are you being that people cannot or will not tell you the truth. Lying always involves two or more people; what is your role in the lie? What is your responsibility in the lie?)

I added the last two pages so that you might have a better idea of what free will looks like. Free will must have discipline, correction, and direction as you develop it over a lifetime. The free will choices of the flesh (mind) will often lead to sin if not controlled. The free will choice of the spirit (heart) will lead you to Jesus. *"Because the carnal mind is enmity against God; for it is not subject to the law of God, nor indeed can be" (Romans 8:7).* Stay conscious of the choices you make because they are not made by accident, or caused by genes. They are free will decisions and God will most certainly hold you fully accountable for every choice you make.

Free will is unique to human beings. Without free will, mankind would be another creature driven by instinct and completely subject to its environment. Mankind is much more than another "mammal" sharing this planet with other creatures, as some scholars would have you believe. God said He created mankind in <u>His</u> image and likeness. In Genesis 1:26, God says, ***"Let Us <u>make</u> man in Our image, according to Our likeness."*** So God made man from the dust of the Earth. In Genesis 1:27, it says, ***"So God <u>created</u> man in His image, in the image of God He created him; male and female He created them."***

So God created man from His Spirit in His image. He did not say this about any other created being. As a matter of fact, mankind is the only creation that God <u>made</u> with His own hands from the dust of the Earth (Genesis 3:19). Everything else God created, He <u>spoke</u> into existence with words, ***"let there be."*** God did not say, "let there be man," no, he made man. He made mankind to dominate this planet and rule over everything on, in, and around it. He made mankind to possess the land and to subdue it. God's plan for mankind always included free will, and with it came a plan to restore him once the (inevitable) choice of evil was made.

Please keep this in mind that God did not create mankind and then watch to see what mankind would do. God is not a reactive Creator. He does not react according to our behavior. On the contrary, our behavior only activates consequences to the set <u>Laws</u> that were in place BEFORE mankind was created. Much like the Earth's gravity does not react to our behavior, but our behavior activates the consequences of ignoring or going against the laws of gravity. It is our bodies that respond to the laws of gravity already in place. God knew exactly what mankind would do with a gift as powerful as free will. He knew mankind would choose evil eventually. Therefore, He created the consequences that would accompany the free will choice of evil. At the same time, God created a means of escape that would free mankind from the consequences of choosing evil.

In the Book of Romans 3:23, it says, ***"for all have sinned and fall short of the glory of God…"*** God's solution was already in place and He would reveal it when the time was right. His original plan for mankind was laid out in Genesis chapters 1 and 2. If mankind had not sinned, then His plan would have been fulfilled as described in Revelation chapters 21 and 22. All that is written in between,

Genesis chapter 3 through Revelation chapter 20 would not have been necessary. By mankind's free will choice of evil, God's plan for forgiveness and restoration was activated. His plan for the salvation of all of mankind is His **phase two** plan.

God had to have a plan for salvation or all of mankind would have had to be destroyed because of sin. Everything that God does is done in an orderly manner, *"Let all things be done decently and in order"* (I Corinthians 14:40). Anything that breaks out of God's order separates itself from God and exposes itself to deadly consequences. Evil or sin has potentially devastating consequences. God warned us in Romans 6:23, *"For the wages of sin is death..."* and summed it all up in James 1:15, *"Then, when desire has conceived, it gives birth to sin; and sin, when it is full-grown, brings forth death."* I'll paraphrase it all by saying that when someone sins, death is assigned to them. Death is always assigned every time sin is committed. Only through repentance is a reprieve from the consequences of sin given. As a born-again believer (a Christian), mankind has the right to repent for sinning. However, without salvation, repentance is not possible because there is no way to access the Father. (Remember, this is a book for believers. If you are not a believer and you want to become a believer, then go back to the end of the Introduction. Read the instructions and say the prayer).

Since mankind had already chosen evil over God in the Garden of Eden, free will was now a reality. Mankind had exercised the free will given to them and chose against the will of God. Now, God would begin to implement His plan for the unavoidable fall of mankind. God also knew mankind was now ready for implementation of the phase two plan.

In the New Testament, in the book of Romans chapter 3, verse 23, states that *"all mankind is sinful."* Again in the Book of Romans chapter 6, verse 23, it states that *"the wages of sin is death."* Another reason these verses were written was to make mankind aware that without the intervention of God in our lives, we will always be defeated by the enemy through sin. Also, to inform us that the desires of the flesh (as opposed to the desires of our spirit), or the desires that are manifested through our five senses will always lead us to defeat

21

and death. In other words, if mankind pursues the carnal desires of the five senses, then they will always be doomed to failure, and death will eventually overtake them.

Just because nothing seems to happen at the time of the sin or crime, does not mean that you have gotten away with it. The consequences for the sin or crime are already in place and they were activated when you sinned. In the book of Ecclesiastes 8:11, it says it like this: *"Because the sentence against an evil work is not executed speedily, therefore the heart of the sons of men [this includes women] is fully set in them to do evil."* Let me say it one more time: Without the intervention of God in your life, you would be doomed to perish from the Earth.

Please keep these things in mind as I continue on. If you are beginning to wonder, just what does all of this have to do with marriage and relationships, I promise you I will pull it all together.

Humanity Under Attack

God's purpose for a phase two plan was to save a remnant of mankind from the death sentence that their sin had brought about. If God had not intervened, then all of mankind would have been lost forever. That was not going to happen, because God had already promised the serpent (in the Garden of Eden) that the "Seed" of the woman would bruise his head. Since God cannot lie, His prophecy had to be fulfilled.

So far, it seems as though God is just an observer. If you read in the sixth chapter of Genesis, you'll find that mankind had become corrupt and evil. *"Then the LORD saw that the wickedness of man was great in the Earth, and that every intent of the thoughts of his heart was only evil continually"* (Genesis 5:6). These were not the human beings that God had created to praise, worship, and serve Him. Their free will had led them so far from God they could not be brought back. *⁶"And the LORD was sorry that He had made man on the Earth, and He was grieved in His heart. ⁷So the LORD said, 'I will destroy man whom I have created from the face of the Earth, both man and beast, creeping thing and birds of the air, for I am sorry that I have made them.'* *⁸But Noah found grace in the eyes of the Lᴏʀᴅ."* (Genesis 6:6-8)

The book of Genesis, chapter 6, describes just how the devil planned to corrupt mankind. (I have to go over this once again because I know there are some of you having trouble accepting this account.) The fallen angels, described as "sons of God," began to [marry] have sex with the daughters of man. Now, keep this in mind, not all of the fallen angels participated. Only those [fallen angels] *"who did not keep their proper domain…"* (Jude 6). The offspring from this unholy relationship were the offspring of the corrupted "seed" of the devil, Satan himself. They were the reason for God's declaration in Genesis 6:6, *"the Lord was sorry that He had made man on the Earth…"* The utter annihilation of these altered half-human beings was necessary in order for God to keep His promise to Satan in the Garden of Paradise, *"that the woman's 'Seed' would bruise his head…"*

Satan's plan was to corrupt all of mankind with his "seed" of evil. The destruction of these half human-spirit and half angelic-spirit creatures left the Earth filled with **demonic** forces capable of depressing, oppressing, and even possessing a human being. I must add at this time that before these things occurred, there were only angels and humans. Now, there was a third type of creature called a demon. There was no such creature before the relationship between the fallen angels and the daughters of man, as described in Genesis 6:1, and now there were <u>millions</u> of these demonic creatures. They virtually covered the Earth.

However, at no time does God allow these demonic creatures to physically touch anyone (unlike the fallen angels). Mankind has to give these demonic forces permission to harm him and even to enter and co-occupy their bodies. There are millions of these creatures because there were millions of people on the Earth at the time of the Flood. People were living for six, seven, eight, and nine hundred years, and producing hundreds of offspring. If one person was affected, all of their offspring would be affected too. The fallen angels would only have to corrupt one generation of people for following generations to be corrupted. The devil thought his plan was nearing completion.

23

(Before I continue on, let me attempt to clear up some loose ends concerning fallen angels.)

Whatever happened to the fallen angels that did not leave their proper abode? Some of the more powerful of the fallen angels were given assignments as the **"principalities, powers, and rulers of darkness, and the forces of spiritual hosts of wickedness in the heavenly places"** (Ephesians 6:12). These are the satanic leaders under which the demons are assigned from region to region throughout the world. They all live in dreaded fear of the power that Jesus has and has given to His Church Body. Those that actually took part in the corruption of mankind (those that left their assigned abode) are bound in chains until the Day of Judgment, *"and the angels who did not keep their proper domain, but left their own abode, He has reserved in everlasting chains under darkness for the judgment of the great day" (Jude 6)*.

If the fallen angels are demonic spirits, then how can they be responsible for depressing, oppressing, and possessing human beings? Jude 6 says, the angels that left their proper domain (or assigned place) are bound with chains until the day of the final judgment. If those that left their proper domain are bound, then they cannot be roaming the planet, causing all the problems that people have endured since the Flood. We know that the devil is only one being, so he cannot be causing all of the problems. Therefore, there must be other creatures that are present on the Earth that were not spoken of in Genesis chapters 1 and 2. These demonic creatures were made on the Earth by mankind and the fallen angels, just as it is stated in Genesis chapter 6. All of the remaining fallen angels are still in their assigned place. They were not bound until the Judgment because they did not sin with mankind. They are still in their assigned places today. The demonic creatures are the offspring of only those that are bound in chains. They were not created like Adam was created, but were made, just as Cain and Abel were made, by the union of mankind.

Demonic forces are the spirit form of the unholy union of mankind and fallen angels, destroyed by the Flood. The angelic spirit and the human spirit produced demonic spirits. These creatures were human-like, while they lived on the Earth, but after they drowned in the Flood, they became spirit-like. These demonic creatures can possess a human being. However, our Bible tells us to "cast out demons," not cast out fallen angels. They were part of Satan's plan to destroy mankind and remove him from the face of the Earth. Satan knew that the "Seed" of the woman could not be born out of corruption, and therefore, he would not have to worry about the birth of the "Seed" from spiritually corrupt beings. The devil was able to destroy all of mankind with the exception of one family of eight people who were not corrupted by these forces. Noah and his family took authority over their desires and were not corrupted with all the rest of humanity.

In Genesis chapter 6, God warned mankind that their days were numbered. God said, *"My Spirit shall not strive with man forever, for he is indeed flesh; yet his days shall be one hundred and twenty years"* (Genesis 6:3). Before this warning, mankind lived into the hundreds, and after the Flood, mankind lived into the hundreds. After the Flood, Noah lived another 350 years, Shem lived another 400 years, and some of his descendents lived for over 400 years. This warning was not about mankind only having a lifespan of 120 years, but it was a warning of impending wrath coming in 120 years for the destruction of mankind because of demonic corruption.

If you cannot believe what I have just told you, then ask yourself who is telling you not to believe it. Read it for yourself in the scriptures; I did. Pray about it and ask the Holy Spirit to give you revelation knowledge concerning these scriptures. The Holy Spirit revealed them to me over four years ago (making of demons). **It really does not matter if you believe what I have written about how demonic forces came into being, but it does matter that you believe that they exist.** They have one purpose and one goal, and that is to steal, kill, and destroy. As born-again believers in Jesus Christ, we have full authority over all the works of the devil. There is power in the name of Jesus, so say the name of Jesus often, but if you don't believe it, then you will not have access to His power.

For every plan of God, Satan has a counterfeit plan, but his plan will always fail because, *"The battle is the Lord's and the victory is ours"* (I Samuel 17:47). God will never lose a battle to the devil. And the devil can never stop you from receiving your victory.

Unfortunately, most Christians either don't know they have spiritual authority over these evil forces or don't believe it. Therefore, they are constantly being attacked and defeated. Many cry out to God for help, but His answer is the same for us today as it was for the Apostle Paul in II Corinthians 12:9: *"my grace is sufficient for you…"* The Apostle Paul said a thorn in the flesh was given to him; he also added that it was a <u>messenger of Satan</u>. He cried out to God three times, but God did not remove his problem, but reminded him that he had the authority to do it himself.

We, too, already have authority over the works of the devil. Jesus said, He came to destroy the works of the devil (I John 3:8). Sounds like the fulfillment of a promise made over 4,000 years ago, in Genesis 3:15: *"and I will put enmity between you and the woman, and between your <u>seed</u> and her <u>Seed</u>; He shall bruise your head, and you shall bruise His heel."* If you do not want to believe that there is a devil, that is your free will choice, but it will not stop the devil from coming to steal, kill, and destroy things in your life. The devil won't leave you alone because you beg God for help either. You must take authority over the works of the devil, just like Paul did. God's grace is truly sufficient for you as a believer today.

Since Satan could not complete his plan to prevent the birth of the "Seed" by corrupting the offspring of humanity, he had to begin the implementation of his phase two plan for deceiving mankind through his lies. Satan is the father of lies (John 8:44). Today his cults have spread all over the Earth. These cults seek spiritual power and pursue it through demonic means. Even the people who are not part of his cults, but deny the existence of God and the deity of His Son Jesus, are being deceived. People will continue to be deceived and led astray, but they too have a free will. They all can perceive good from bad and right from wrong. They know what evil is and certainly know there is a God. It is their choice to serve the devil here on Earth, and it is their choice to burn with him in the lake of fire for all eternity after the Judgment.

Satan is only a single being. He cannot be in more than one place at a time. His evil forces, demonic spirits, are what most people encounter on a daily basis. People say that they have seen ghosts. They say that some psychic told them about the future. They are actually seeing demonic spirits and talking to people that are aligned with demonic spirits. No one returns from the dead; they remain there until the Judgment Day. Hebrews 9:27 says, *"and as it is appointed for men to die once, but after this the judgment,"* and Psalms 78:39 says, *"For He remembered that they were but flesh, a breath that passes away and does not come again."* If you are using 1-900 dial-a-psychic, you need to know that they are in league with the devil. They can only tell you about things that have already happened because the demons know your past, but they cannot tell you the future because the demons have not been there. Only God can tell you the future and He uses prophets to send you those messages.

I cannot believe all the excitement over psychics. They tell you your grandmother's name and your address and you get all excited. Did you know your grandmother's name and your address before they told you? So, what did they tell you or what can they tell you that you do not already know about your past? What I cannot believe is so-called Christians call these numbers, read their horrible scopes and even believe in them. What Jesus do you believe in? What Bible are you reading? Who is your source, God or Satan? Do not be deceived by their lies. Remember, when you sin, death is assigned to you.

I hope the first two chapters of this book have laid the foundation for marriage and relationships. God loves people from the moment of their conception until the moment of their death. He will not stop loving all of mankind, even those practicing evil. He gives everyone the opportunity to come to Him through His Son, Jesus, right up to their last breath. God wants a personal relationship with all of mankind. It is His desire for all of mankind to be saved through believing in His Son, Jesus, but God will NOT interfere with the free will of any human being that He has created. God did not stop Adam and Eve from sinning in the Garden of Eden and He will not stop you.

Exercise your free will and choose life, choose Jesus. *"Jesus is the way the truth and the life, no one comes to the Father, except through Me"* (John 14:6). If you do choose Jesus, then God's grace will be sufficient for you to defeat the attacks of the devil and thereby, live a long, prosperous, and peaceful life.

God said, *"My people are destroyed for lack of knowledge"* (Hosea 4:6). Marriages are destroyed for a lack of knowledge. There are thousands of books, articles, and teaching on marriage. However, the knowledge in most of these books won't help your marriage. The answers that you are seeking are not in those books. Many are filled with the knowledge of man, but lack the wisdom of God. For most people, even in the Church, the Bible is the last place they look to find the answers they need. They refuse to trust God, because they have not developed a personal relationship with His Son, Jesus. They know about God, but they don't know Him. They trust what they hear in the secular world and believe the soap operas, movies, and talk shows. They are seeking answers in a world that is lost in fleshly desires and sinful pursuits. If you want treatment, then go to the world. The world is full of treatment programs. However, if you want healing, for any problem or affliction, come to Jesus. Jesus is THE healer. Besides, you will not find any treatment programs in the Bible.

Do you want you marriage healed or treated? Do you want your family restored or just counseled? Do you want love, joy, peace, patience, kindness, goodness, gentleness, faithfulness, and self-discipline in your marriage and in your life? The choice, as always, is up to you. **When given the choice of life or death, choose life!** (Deuteronomy 31:19 paraphrased)

You don't have to hit bottom before you decide to make some permanent changes in your life. God has a plan and a purpose for your life. Have you noticed that God's plan always succeeds? The attacks will come, but they cannot last or win without help from you. God already has a plan for escape and a plan for victory whenever you are attacked.

God's plan for Satan and his cohorts is already set in stone. They will be thrown into the fires of hell. Keep this in mind whenever you are being attacked because it will remind you that the victory is yours. God's plan will keep you on the road to self-worth. Don't alter God's plan for your life. Just follow it to the end by faith.

Praise the Lord!

***

CHAPTER THREE
GOD'S ORDER

"Let all things be done decently and in order."
(I Corinthians 14:40)

So far, we have covered the plan of God with phases one and two, and the plan of Satan, phases one and two. By now, Satan is fit to be tied because he almost succeeded on two different occasions to eliminate mankind from the face of the Earth. First, he enticed Cain to murder Abel, and if he could have tricked him into murdering Eve, all humanity would have ended. Next, he contaminated the entire Earth's population with his evil seed. He only had eight people remaining to corrupt before the entire Earth was his once again. Since he failed in that attempt, he had to stand by and watch Noah's family repopulate the Earth. Now, he knew he had to act fast before one of the remaining women gave birth to the "Seed" that would destroy him. So what could he possibly do now?

While Satan was trying to figure out exactly what he would do next, God had already begun to act. He wasn't just a few months or years ahead of the devil, He was 500 years ahead of him. Five hundred years after the birth of Noah, God began to fully implement phase two of His original plan for mankind. It is important for you to know that the story of Noah is not only truly stated, but it is also a statement of truth. It is the first of five key pivotal points in the Bible that came after the fall of mankind. These five points are defining events that would usher in the millennial reign of Jesus and the final coming together of the Body of Christ. They are:

1. the remnant of humanity—the seed of Noah and his family
2. the faith of Abraham
3. the birth, death, and resurrection of Jesus
4. the establishment of the Body of Christ, which is Christianity
5. the worldwide spread of the Gospel for the return of Jesus

God's new order for mankind in phase two began with four couples: Noah, his three sons, and each of their wives. With Noah and his family, God re-established His principles for marriage (Adam and Eve being the first married couple.). Each man had one wife and one wife only (God knew man would be in over his head with more than one wife). God's plan for marriage is clear, it is an exclusive relationship between one man and one woman. This marriage foundation also established God's desire for a one-on-one relationship between Himself and mankind. God's ultimate phase two plan for mankind is a personal relationship with Him, through His Son, Jesus.

Family Under Attack

There was truly a man named Noah and he had a wife and three married sons. Also, there were millions of people living on the Earth at this time. Of all the people living on the Earth, only Noah and his family had not been corrupted by the devil's plan for the destruction of mankind, (Genesis 6:12) *"for all flesh had corrupted their way on the Earth."* However, it did appear that the devil's plan was very near to being completed. Then, when things looked their worst, God intervened and began to implement His own plan.

When Noah was about 500 years old, God spoke to him and told him to build an ark. God gave him the directions for this ark because no one had ever considered such a thing. The ark, when completed, would house Noah and his wife, his three sons and their wives. It would also house animals, birds, and insects. You can just imagine how enormous this ark must have been. It took Noah 100 years to complete this project. Noah was 500 years old when he started to build the Ark. He also, was 500 years old when God gave him and his wife three sons, triplets, that he named Shem, Ham, and Japheth. By the time the ark was finally ready, 100 years later, Noah's sons had found wives and were married.

Now, God told Noah to enter the ark with his family and He closed the door behind him. I am sure that there must have been people pounding on the door and climbing onto the outer shell of the ark as the water began to rise. It would be to no avail, because the death sentence that had been assigned to them, for their sins and wickedness, had finally caught up with them. With the sealing of the ark, the devil's plan was thwarted once again and God's plan for phase two of mankind had begun.

(On that fateful day people were still sinning and living their lives in complete oblivion to the impending wrath of God. On that day the consequences of sin was painfully obvious. However, it was too late to repent, to change, or to escape. This is an example and a warning for the final day of the End Times. God's wrath will be unimaginable. His warning has been written down and sent, not 120 years in advance, but 2000 years in advance. On that final day it will be once again too late to repent, to change, or to escape.)

One hundred years before that fateful day, when Noah was 500 years old, God began to prepare him for his escape from the coming wrath. Noah and his wife did not have any children then. His sons were born that year, and during the next 100 years, they grew and even found wives for themselves. Their wives were from the daughters of mankind who were <u>not</u> corrupted by fallen angels.

There must have been others besides Noah who could have listened to the warning and turned away from evil and walked with God. ***"This is the genealogy of Noah. Noah was a just man, perfect in his generations. Noah <u>walked with God</u>"*** (Genesis 6:9). There could have been more than the eight people saved in the Ark, if they had heeded God's warning. In the end, only three of the daughters of man who married Noah's sons escaped God's wrath with Noah's family. Since the daughters were not corrupted at the time of their marriages, their parents were probably not corrupted at that time also. However, their parents and their siblings did not remain that way.

As it is stated in Genesis chapter 6, it rained for forty days and forty nights. Everything that lived on the surface of the Earth was destroyed. Noah and his family spent the next year in the ark. After forty days and nights of rain, it took one year, two months, and ten days for the Earth to dry out enough for Noah, his family, and the animals to once again leave the ark. Once all the Noah and all the creatures had departed the ark, they all began to do what God had commanded them to do: reproduce, multiply, and replenish the Earth.

Additionally, since the Earth's land surface was still attached together, the animals could wander to the four corners of the Earth. It wasn't until years later, approximately three generations that the Earth's surface was divided up into continents (Genesis 10:25): *"To Eber were born two sons: the name of one was Peleg, for in his days the Earth was divided..."* It would not be long afterward that the children of Noah would be divided into nations too. God was about to begin anew. His plan for the coming of His "Seed" was right on schedule.

There is one more important point that I must make to put things into the right perspective. Mankind was not destroyed just because of sin. Noah and his sons and their families still had the sin of Adam, and there was no way of getting rid of it at that time. However, Noah had God's grace (Genesis 6:8), and God found him righteous in his generation (Genesis 7:1). I believe that Noah, just like Enoch, repented for their sins and for the iniquity of their fathers and found favor in the eyes of God. So, it wasn't just a sin issue, but an issue of sin at a level that became an abomination in the sight of God.

In the ten generations from Adam to Noah, when mankind lived an average of 850 years, humanity went from God's enlightenment to Satan's darkness. Adam and Eve knew God personally. They were the most brilliant creatures on the Earth and their brilliance waned with each succeeding generation. In Adam's time, mankind knew God and they knew how to serve Him. Both Cain and Abel knew how to serve God because their father taught them. Cain chose evil and God separated him from his family. When he departed, iniquity followed after him.

However, in Noah's time, mankind knew evil all the time. They no longer served God or followed His ways. The Bible says in Hebrews 6:4-5: *"For it is impossible for those who were once enlightened, and have tasted the heavenly gift, and have become partakers of the Holy Spirit, and have tasted the good word of God and the powers of the age to come, if they fall away, to renew them again to repentance..."* (Satan and the fallen angels) By the time of Noah's generation, mankind had grown so far away from God that repentance was not possible and forgiveness was not available from God.

The corruption of mankind with evil and the attempt by the devil to prevent the coming of the "Seed" of the woman was still the primary focus of Satan. The "Seed" was certainly going to come because God said it, and that made it so. The sin of mankind from Adam was already in God's plan from the beginning, because sin is the dark side of free will. The "Seed" would, of course, eventually redeem mankind and set them free. However, the "Seed" was not coming to stop mankind from sinning. It takes an act of our free will not to sin. The "Seed" was coming to restore the choice of God and eternal life with God to all of mankind. The free will choice of mankind in the time of Noah was to sin willfully because of their corruption and evil nature. However, God only needs a seed, a remnant, to produce a harvest of righteousness. Out of the millions of people on the Earth, God only needed the seed of Noah and seven others to replenish the Earth with people.

Noah and his family were not pervasive in sinning like the rest of the world, but they did have sin in their lives. I just want to point out the character of God in dealing with mankind. He is patient and His mercy endures forever to those who diligently seek Him. God will not tolerate willful sinning forever. When it reaches its limit (preset by God) then it will trigger His wrath. This clearly happened in Sodom and Gomorrah. Remember, when we sin, death is assigned to us. Noah and his family weren't lucky or special. They freely choose to keep away from corruption. God is no respecter of persons, but He is a respecter of faith in His Word. I am sure that it wasn't easy to stand against the tide of world opinion, but Noah did. Even if the entire world disagrees with you, stand on the Word of God.

Soon after the flood waters receded, Noah and his family members began to rebuild their lives. Their adversary, the devil, did not lose his focus on them for one minute. There were only eight people, and four of them were female. He was not about to allow them to begin to give birth. He knew it would only be a matter of time before one of them would give birth to the "Seed" that he lived in fear of since the birth of Cain. Again, he had to introduce a diversion from their everyday life, something that they would not be expecting. Once again, the devil's attack would be directed at the relationship between mankind and God first and against the relationship between man and woman secondly.

Genesis 9:20-24: *"And Noah began to be a farmer, and he planted a vineyard. [21]Then he drank of the wine and was drunk, and became uncovered in his tent. [22]And Ham, the father of Canaan, saw the nakedness of his father, and told his two brothers outside. [23]But Shem and Japheth took a garment, laid it on both their shoulders, and went backward and covered the nakedness of their father. Their faces were turned away, and they did not see their father's nakedness. [24]So Noah awoke from his wine, and knew what his younger son had done to him."*

How many times have you read that passage and wondered why there was all the fuss over Ham seeing his father's nakedness? I would imagine that during the 100 years that Ham had been alive and living with his father, that he and his brothers had seen each other naked on many occasions. So why was this time such a big deal? I did not see it until I had read the Book of Leviticus a number of times. In chapter 18, the word "nakedness" is used thirty-one times. (Leviticus 18: 6, *"None of you shall approach anyone who is near of kin to him, to uncover his nakedness…"* and verse 7, *"The nakedness of your father or the nakedness of your mother you shall not uncover…"* etc.) Each time it is used, it is in conjunction with sexual sins. It still did not dawn on me what nakedness really meant in Genesis 9, even after reading and understanding what Moses was talking about in the Book of Leviticus. However, when I read that Noah cursed Canaan instead of Ham after the incident, then it made me stop and think about what was actually going on.

Why would Noah curse Canaan instead of Ham who "saw" him naked? Canaan was Ham's son and therefore, Noah's grandson. Noah could not curse Ham because God had blessed him, along with his brothers and their wives in Genesis 9:1, *"So God blessed Noah and his sons, and said to them: Be fruitful and multiply and fill the Earth."* Noah knew that you never curse anyone that God had blessed. Therefore he cursed his grandson, Canaan. So why curse anyone for seeing him naked? It wasn't a matter of seeing, but of what he did to him. Ham committed the first recorded homosexual act in the Bible. It was a grievous act as far as God was concerned, and Noah knew it. By cursing Canaan, Noah hoped to stop the iniquity of Ham's sin from being passed down to the generation that followed.

(Let me clarify one very important point, and that is homosexuality is a sin, an act, and not a person. The sin is an abomination in the eyes of God, not people. Hate the sin, because God does, but love the people.)

God had commanded Noah and his family to *"Be fruitful and multiply and fill the Earth."* How can a homosexual act be fruitful or productive to humanity, or be used to multiply and fill the Earth? It cannot produce anything productive and humanity certainly cannot be multiplied by homosexuality. Just as mankind was given a new lease on life, sin at a great magnitude entered their lives. Homosexuality is a truly egregious act in the sight of God and man. Who do you think could be behind such a thing? The Bible says that *"the serpent was more cunning than any beast of the field..."* (Genesis 3:1). Satan used a serpent to disguise himself in order to deceive Eve. This time he used mankind's sexual desire, perverted it, and used it to try to bring about the final destruction of all mankind.

Once again, mankind was caught off guard. Now that Canaan was cursed, the devil knew he did not have to worry about the "Seed" coming from his descendants. In Genesis chapter 19, the cities of Sodom and Gomorrah and all the cities of Canaan were destroyed by fire and brimstone that rained down from heaven. The primary sin of the inhabitants of those cities was homosexuality. The wrath of God did pour down on mankind for their homosexuality, but not the way Satan had planned. The other descendants of Ham were not cursed by anyone and they did spread throughout the regions assigned to them, multiplying and filling the Earth.

I suppose in the days before the Flood that homosexuality was being practiced, because the Lord said in Genesis 6:5-6 that the wickedness of man was great and that He was sorry that he had made man. Noah and his family were exposed to the wickedness of mankind every day while they worked on the ark. I am sure they knew about sin and they made a conscious choice not to participate in man's depravity.

The Bible says the Noah found grace in the eyes of God. You would think that after living through the Flood and being given the opportunity to begin anew that all of Noah's family would have stayed far away from sin. After all, they were the seeds of a new order of mankind that would one day produce the salvation of all mankind. God is merciful and His mercy endures forever. He is a patient God and He withheld His wrath, when it would have been justified to pour it out. He knew that mankind was doing the best it could do at the time and in due season, mankind would win.

The Word of God is true: *"all have sinned and fall short of the glory of God"* (Romans 3:23). Noah and his family did not have a covenant with God. The Israelites had a covenant with God, The Old Testament, and yet sin continued. The Ten Commandments and Law could not stop mankind from sinning. Today, God has given you a better Covenant through His Son, Jesus, yet sin still abounds. Sin will continue to abound because the conditions of our free will have not changed. The choice is still the same, choose God or evil. You can believe the world and all of its secular babble or you can believe the Word of God. Only through The Law of the New Covenant which is LOVE can we hope to triumph over sin.

Spiritual Warfare and Sin

In the Gospel of Luke 1:35, God reveals that the "Seed" will come from the Holy Spirit. The "Seed" is Jesus, the Son of God. He was sent to restore mankind to his rightful place. The Bible goes on to tell us, *"Before I formed you in the womb I knew you; before you were born I sanctified you…"* (Jeremiah 1:5). The restoration of mankind was planned before God created them. The answer to the fall of Adam and Eve was already set before they were created. Satan knew Jesus was the coming "Seed" because he saw Him in heaven before he was cast out of heaven. In Luke 10:18, Jesus tells us, *"I saw Satan fall like lightning from heaven. Behold, I give you the authority to trample on serpents and scorpions, and over all the*

39

power of the enemy [Satan] and nothing shall by any means hurt you. Nevertheless, do not rejoice in this, that the [evil] spirits are subject to you, but rather rejoice because your names are written in heaven." Even as Satan found out about God's plan, he never had the power to stop God's plan.

Let's look again at the relationship between the fallen angels and mankind, in hope of bringing a little more clarity to the situation. I believe many Christians are still very skeptical about these demonic forces and where they came from. It is important to be clear because of the tremendous impact that these forces can have on you as a human being and on your marriage and relationship with God.

Since these demons are part human, they can possess human beings; however, they must have your permission. In the Gospel of Mark 5:1-20, Jesus tells us that He cast out "Legion" with his 2,000 cohorts from the wild man of Gadarenes. When Jesus cast them out, they asked permission to enter the swine on the hillside. Jesus allowed them to enter the swine. They could not even possess the swine without permission. You have to give demonic forces permission to possess you as well as defeat you. You have authority over all demonic forces and fallen angels that may come against you. However, if you do not know about your authority and power, then you certainly can not exercise it over them.

Please understand that the demonic forces that were created were a part of the devil's plan to stop the coming of the Messiah, Jesus Christ. Jesus is the "Seed" of the woman and the devil knew it. God circumvented the devil's plan, as always, and set mankind back on track to fulfill his destiny through Noah. Do not think for one minute that the devil has given up on the destruction of mankind. He continues to attack families, marriages, and individuals as the opportunities present themselves. *"The thief [devil] comes to steal, kill and destroy. However, Jesus has come to give us life and life more abundantly"* (John 10:10). Call on the name of Jesus each and every time you believe you are under an attack of the enemy.

Understanding the nature of the spiritual warfare attacks that may be waged against you each day is paramount to your having the ability to defeat them. If you could only see the demonic forces as they are approaching your families, marriages, and yourselves, then you would focus your counterattack on these forces and not on other people. Pastors and lay counselors would no longer hear about what he or she (my spouse) made me do; or what they (other people) did to me. You would know it is another attack of the enemy against you. Then spouses, in particular, would join together and put 10,000 (demonic forces) to flight as the Bible tells us to do. The Christian divorce rate would drop to zero because people would stop giving up in the midst of the fight, and stand together until the victory is manifested. (I'll talk more about this in a later chapter.)

All of Satan's phase one and phase two planning could not stop what God had already put in place. I have taken the time to lay the foundation of this spiritual warfare (over and over again), so that you know exactly what you are up against when demonic attacks are manifested. You are commanded to believe in God's Word. You are commanded to have faith in His Word and not be moved by the lies and deceit of the enemy. As you read on in this book, keep in mind the foundation of who you are as a Christian. You are a believer and a disciple of Jesus Christ. You are in the world, but you are not of the world.

This book is written for primarily for "disciples" and for believers. There are no treatment programs for the demonic attacks that come against your health, your mind, your marriage, or your relationships found in the Bible. Jesus is a healer. If you want your marriage healed or your family restored, then call on the name of Jesus. If you want treatment programs, then call on the world's system. Be clear about who the enemy is and where the attacks are coming from.

In the book of Deuteronomy 31:19, it says (paraphrased) given the choice of life or death, choose life. God told us what to choose so that we would not be confused when the time for making the choice became available to us. Satan has disguised death in many ways so that we are often deceived. Today, he has elevated man's desire for things of the flesh to such a level that people actually believe that if it feels good, it **is** all right to do it. There is even a disregard for human rights and an elevation in the focus on animal rights, nature's rights, and even the "right" to die.

Today, the command to <u>choose life</u> is barely an echo in our memories. Why choose life when death seems so appealing? Why fight for a marriage when a divorce is so easily obtained? Why raise your own children when you believe it "takes a village" to do it right? (A village cannot raise your children because it's full of idiots today. It is full of amoral degenerates looking for opportunities to prey on your children.) It takes parents that serve the Lord and keep His commandants to raise their children. It takes a Jesus-lead church body to support families in raising their children. Satan will use anything that is against the will of God to distract us and confuse us. No matter how idiotic it may be, people will choose death and every form of it because they have surrendered their free will to the enemy, the devil. They will even fight for the "right to die" when being led by the devil.

I hope that you have become more aware of the real battle that is being waged against you. The ultimate target is your relationship with God, and then your relationship with others, especially with your spouse. This is what spiritual warfare looks like up close and personal. The all-out assault on marriage is a plan of Satan. He knows the Messiah has already come on the Earth, so now his focus is to steal, kill, and destroy everything from anybody that will allow him into their lives.

The battle is not against your spouse, but it is against you. If you knew what the Word of God said about marriage and relationships, would you follow it? I believe that most Christians do not know what the Word of God says about marriage. They follow the world's teaching and get the world's results. I hope as you continue on that you will receive God's Word on marriage, because it is His creation. If you do it God's way, your marriage MUST work, because God cannot lie. If you trust in God through His Son, Jesus, by being in relationship with Him, you will be successful in your marriage and in all of your relationships.

I hope that I have not been too redundant about the plans of Satan in these first three chapters. Some of what I have written is controversial, but do not get stuck there. You will believe whatever you choose, and no one can make another person believe anything that they don't want to believe. I just want to make sure that you are equipped and prepared to understand the model for marriage and relationships that I will begin to discuss in chapter four.

Marriage is too precious to be thrown away at the alarming rate that it is today. Instead of focusing on the enemy, the devil, too many spouses focus on each other as the enemy. I pray that you will no longer be deceived, and more than that, that you will now recognize that the attack against your marriage is planned. The attack is spiritual warfare, so don't make it personal, and especially don't make it physical. There will always be opportunities for attacks against you, but these attacks should NEVER defeat you.

There are scriptures to show that God did create the angels and mankind; however, there are no scriptures to show that God created demons. There are millions of demons, but there are many more millions of humans. Because of this, demonic forces must rely on fear, self-doubt, low self-worth, and your wrong thinking to do much of the work for them. Evangelist Joyce Meyer is right when she says the battlefield is in the mind. That is good news, because God said that He has given you a sound mind. All you have to do is use it.

God's Word says that we can transform and even renew our minds. God's Word says that we can bring every thought into captivity to the obedience of Christ Jesus. All you have to do is to do it, in the name of Jesus. Don't accept defeat by believing you have lost. No, the only way to lose is for you to quit. Jesus will never leave you; He will be right there 24/7. Just call on Him, don't beg Him or whine to Him. Be bold and confident and courageous in who you are in Christ Jesus.

Remember, the battle is the Lord's and the victory is yours. Stop trying to fight in the flesh; arm yourself as in Ephesians chapter 6 and fight as in II Corinthians 10:3-6. God has order in everything that He does. He created mankind to be superior to fallen angels as well as demonic creatures. You will one day judge the fallen angels. It is up to all of mankind to take that authority. God has done His part and now it is up to the Body of Christ to do their part in spreading the Word of God, the Gospel of Jesus Christ.

Before you read chapter four and see God's plan for your marriage and relationships, decide right now that your word is your bond. The vow you made is forever to both your spouse and to God. You gave your word, now stand on it. Now read on and see the goodness that the Lord has for your marriage.

Praise the Lord!

***

CHAPTER FOUR
MARRIAGE

"Marriage is honorable among all"
(Hebrews 13:4)

In spite of all of Satan's efforts, millions of human beings chose Jesus and are still choosing Him. Because of the woman, the "Seed" of God did come to the Earth and Satan's hatred for women was magnified. Because of God's blessings on marriage and the power given to the head of the household, Satan hates marriage and family intensely. He will not relinquish his attacks on mankind. Marriages will always be under full-scale attack of the enemy. Those who choose to follow the Word of God on marriage by obtaining the knowledge, understanding, and wisdom necessary for a successful marriage will experience all of the tremendous blessings that God has prepared for Christian spouses. Those who choose not to pursue God's Word will suffer and be defeated time and time again.

A relationship with God through His Son, Jesus, is paramount for mankind to enjoy life on this planet. The more knowledge, understanding, and wisdom that you can obtain from God's Word for marriage, the greater the rewards will be for your life on the Earth. Mankind was not put on the Earth to suffer until death and then and only then enjoy the magnitude of God's blessings once they were in heaven. No, God's blessings are available to you right now on Earth. Being married is a blessing and it should get better and better every day, because it was established by God. If you do not lose sight of the fact that there is a spiritual warfare battle going on against your marriage and against your family, then you will be better equipped to deal with it, defeat the attacks, and destroy the works of the demonic forces that have come against you.

If you are a Christian, then live your life according to the Word of God. Marriage is honorable in the eyes of God. Be married according the Word of God and not according to some secular study or the latest theory on marriage. There are no theories in the Bible; if you want theories, then go to the world's system. If you want a successful marriage, then come to Jesus. Jesus **is** the answer to everything you need. His love will conquer all.

Marriage God's Way

"Two are better than one, because they have a good reward for their labor, for if they fall, one will lift up his companion. But woe to him who is alone when he falls, for he has no one to help him up... And a threefold cord is not quickly broken." Ecclesiastes 4:9-10, 12b NKJ

Marriage is the union of two people, a **man** and a **woman**. It is not a union between a <u>male</u> and a <u>female</u>. A male and a female have to make a free will choice to become a man and a woman. A man and a woman can become a father and a mother, but a male and a female can never become a father and a mother. God said that He created them male and female, in other words <u>every</u> human being is born as either a male or a female. God did not make mistakes and give some the wrong bodies. You are first and foremost a spirit that lives within a body. That body is a perfect match for the spirit that you are. However, God did give you the right to reject even yourselves, your body, and to make any free will choice you want concerning your life and lifestyle. You can believe God or the latest scientific theory. It is up to you.

It is important to recognize the truth, the Word of God, as opposed to the lies of the devil. (Now do you see why the foundation for spiritual warfare with its demonic activity was necessary?) A male can marry another male or may attempt to become a female by changing body parts. A male can be sexually attracted to a child or an animal, or who knows what else, and the same is true for a female. However, a man can never marry another man. He would never change body parts and attempt to become a female or be a sexual deviant, and the same is true for a woman. The truth is that God made mankind in His Image and Likeness. You have the ability to make a free will choice to pursue God or pursue evil with all of its perversions.

Marriage is God's creation. Along with His creation of marriage came instructions on how to live in it. If you choose to follow His instructions, then you will (I said *will*) have a blessed and highly successful marriage. If you choose to be married in some other way, by some other standard, then expect to have the opposite results.

It is disgusting to see so many Christian marriages ending in divorce, including those who are called into the fivefold ministry by God, and who say that they know the Word of God. Let me add that even those called into the fivefold ministry by God cannot interfere with the free will choice of their spouses, if their spouse decides to divorce. I am not talking about that, but I am talking about those who say that God told them to divorce their spouse and to marry someone else. What utter nonsense! Their excuse is that they chose the wrong person and God is correcting their mistake. How can God speak against His own Word? Jesus said a house divided against itself cannot stand. How can God create marriage and give instructions for the success of that marriage, and then tell someone that He made a mistake? If you choose to divorce, then divorce, but stop blaming God for your free will choice and your sin.

When you marry according to the Word of God, then you have formed a threefold cord. The threefold cord is you, your spouse, and the Holy Spirit. This threefold union was established when you vowed to be married. The vow of marriage is made horizontally to each other, then vertically to God. Stating a vow or giving your word is what establishes the marriage. Marriage, like everything else, is established first in the natural by speaking it to your spouse and then in the spiritual world by speaking it to God. *"When you make a vow to God, do not delay to pay it; for He has no pleasure in fools. Pay what you have vowed—⁵Better not to vow than to vow and not pay. ⁶Do not let your mouth cause your flesh to sin nor say before the messenger of God that it was an error"* (Ecclesiastes 5:4-6). The vows you made are forever. If you don't believe you can be married forever (to the same person), then don't make the vow. If you do, then God says that you are a fool. Stand on truth of the Word of God and not foolishness.

God has laid out a blueprint for marriage. He knew how difficult it could be for two people to be married to each other without having instructions on how to make it work. I started this book out with the foundation that God put in place for marriage and the attack that was being established against it. I felt that it was important to know and understand the tremendous amount time the devil puts in trying to destroy marriages and relationships that God has established. If you think that marriage is a hit-or-miss affair, then why not keep marrying and divorcing until you get it right (which will be never)? However, if you know that you are in the right marriage from the start and there is no other person for you, then your decisions about your marriage will work for you and not against you.

If God established marriage to last for your lifetime, then it cannot get worse over the years; it has to get better with time. The three-year itch and the seven-year itch are figments of the world's imagination. Without God in your marriage, with His instructions on marriage, you marriage won't be successful. Be completely confident in this that God established the marriage covenant and therefore, it must work.

So where is this blueprint for marriage? Go and get your Bible, then turn to the Book of Ephesians chapter 5:22-33 and 6:1-4. *"Wives, submit to your own husbands, as to the Lord. ²³For the husband is head of the wife, as also Christ is head of the church; and He is the Savior of the body. ²⁴Therefore, just as the church is subject to Christ, so let the wives be to their own husbands in everything."*

I think back on the number of times that I read this passage and did not understand it as the blueprint for marriage. I liked the part about "wives, submit to your own husbands" and the part about the husband as head of the wife. It did not dawn on me to include the next part of those verses that say "as to the Lord" and "as also Christ is head of the church." Now that gives a different meaning to everything. A wife's submission "as to the Lord" and a husband's headship as Christ is the head of the church was a direct assault on my belief system. I needed transformation and renewing of my mind in these areas. I thought that women were subject to men and because of that, women had no real say or authority in the marriage. I was certainly wrong and I already had the experience of divorce to prove it.

The very next verse really opened my eyes. Verse 25 says, ***"Husbands _love_ your wives, just as Christ also loved the church and gave Himself for her."*** It was as if a light had finally come on in my head and heart. I realized, for the first time in my life, that I had not **loved** my wife in my previous marriage. Actually, I had been married twice before. Once when I was twenty-three and that marriage lasted six years, and again when I was thirty-four, and this time it lasted for eleven years. Yes, I had been married and divorced twice by the time I was forty-six years young. I did not love either one of my wives because I did not understand what love was all about. I had physical lust for them, so I thought that must mean that I still loved them. The confusing thing was that I had physical lust for most women, so what did that mean? I finally came to the conclusion that marriage was not for me, because it just did not work.

I have to admit that after reading and finally receiving some understanding of Ephesians 5:22-25, I was excited about marriage again. I knew that my parents were married for fifty years, so they must have done something right. I had always felt like a failure and a disappointment to them because of my divorces. Now, I knew what to do so that my next marriage could actually work. I had to LOVE my wife.

I remember asking this question over and over to the Lord, you mean that if I love my wife, my marriage can really work? You mean, Lord, that is all there is to it. I was really excited, because I did want to get married again. I did not want to continue to barhop and meet different women for one-night stands, because I knew I was sinning. I was fornicating and committing adultery with different women that I knew I would never marry. I am not saying fornication or adultery is justified because you plan to marry later. No, sin has no justification.

I had already begun to feel convicted by my behavior, but I did not know how I was going to stop. I had always justified my behavior by saying to myself that as long as we are both willing partners, then it cannot be wrong. It was more than wrong, it was sin. I did not care if the woman was married. I bought into the saying that he (the husband) must be doing something wrong for his wife to be out there looking for sex outside of their marriage. If she was willing, then I was willing. What nonsense! I was 100 percent responsible for my behavior regardless of what anyone else wanted or did.

God's Hand Is on Your Life

Let me go back a few years to the day that I was finally born-again. It was November 20, 1988. I had been asked, no hounded, by a Navy lieutenant to attend church with him and his family for almost two years. I still do not know why I said yes on that particular Sunday, but I am thankful that he did not give up on me. Oh, by the way, I was a Command Master Chief in the U.S. Navy at the time and I was not a very approachable person. I know that I gave him a hard time for asking me, because I did not want to hear about Jesus. I was raised Catholic and I had not gone to church very often over the last ten years.

Anyhow, I went to church with him and met the pastor, Wayne Speer. I don't remember much about the sermon or the service, but the fellowship after the service got my attention. The pastor said to me, if I needed anything, just stop by anytime day or night. Later that evening, as I was preparing to go out to my favorite nightclub, I remembered what he had said. It was around 10:00 P.M. and I decided to stop by his home and see if he meant what he said. I knocked on the door and his wife answered. I told her that I had been in the service that morning and the pastor told me to stop by anytime, day or night, if I needed anything. She said for me to wait a minute, closed the door, and walked away. I thought she would come back and say that the pastor was sleeping and come back tomorrow. That would have supported my belief that this Christian thing was just talk. However, the pastor came to the door and invited me in.

As they say, the rest is history. I received the Lord Jesus Christ as my Lord and Savior that night. The pastor told me and showed me things in the Bible that I had never heard of before. When he showed me Romans 10:9-10, I couldn't believe it at first. I thought that's all I have to do to be saved. Of course, I confessed Jesus as my Lord and Savior. I always believed that Jesus was the Son of God. I repented for my sins and I left his home feeling like I weighed only five pounds. I had just made a 180-degree turn in my life. **The turn was easy, but the rough road of transformation and renewing of my mind was just beginning**. I had made my turn onto the road *to* self-worth.

I saw Pastor Wayne one other time, two days later on Tuesday, November 22. He baptized me in Kaneohe Bay, Hawaii at 6:00 in the morning. I never saw him again after that. He was transferred to Europe by his denomination. He did leave me a Bible, and I still have it today. He wrote an inscription in it and it has blessed my life to this day; **"Please always read and study His Word, so you may become more like Jesus everyday. May He bless you in <u>direct proportion</u> to your <u>service</u> to Him."** He signed it Wayne Speer, a servant of Jesus. It wasn't until a few years later that I began to understand the significance of God's blessing in direct proportion to my service to Him.

I thought I should share my testimony with you because I did not begin to have conviction concerning my sinful life on my own. I knew all about sin from my Catholic upbringing, but I never let that stop me from doing whatever I wanted to do. It was only after I had been saved that I had the conviction of the Holy Spirit every time I even thought of sinning. God had begun to do a new work within me. The Lord began with my relationship with women because I had hurt them the most. There were many other areas of my life that He could have begun with, such as:

- My drinking (I was drinking every night, up to a case of beer or a fifth of booze in an evening on far too many occasions.)

- My smoking (I had smoked 2-3 packs/day for twenty-two years; I had quit almost two years earlier, but the craving was still there.)

- My gambling (I was fully addicted and out of control with tens of thousands of dollars in gambling loses and debts.)

- My foul language, lack of compassion for people, pride, arrogance, and anger (I was heading for a heart-attack or stroke.)

- I had a "sorry, I'm too busy" relationship with my eighteen-year-old son (I had never been there for him, from the time he was four until he was eighteen years old.)

- I had a totally out-of-sight, out-of-mind nonexistent relationship with my ten-year-old daughter (another female); (I saw her for the first time when she was eleven years old.)

- I harbored an ongoing animosity towards the mothers of my children. (I wanted nothing to do with either of them.)

The Lord knew where to start with me. He showed me the lack of respect I had for women; of course, I thought I had the utmost respect for them. More importantly, He showed the lack of respect I had for myself as a man. Husbands, love your wives as Christ loves the Church, now that was a wake up call for me. I knew immediately that I had never loved my first or second wife. I guess in the world view, my feelings for my wives could have been construed as love, but now I know better. All I really had for them was lust, sexual lust. I had no idea there was a difference. I thought as long as I was still sexually attracted, then I must still love them. Now I know that is the world view. However, I found out from the Word of God that love has nothing whatsoever to do with feelings or emotions, period. Love isn't feelings and it's certainly not thoughts, but it is acting on what you say.

I did not make any remarkable changes overnight, but I was keenly aware of my actions and behavior around women. I felt the conviction and I truly wanted to change, but many times I felt powerless to do anything about it. I would still go out to nightclubs, but now I was looking for a wife and not a one-night stand. I was also conscious of the fact that I did not know what love really was or how to get it. I questioned how I would be able to love someone else just for who they are and not for what they brought to the relationship for me. I found that I was still looking for someone to love me, someone I could trust. I still did not know how I was going to love them or trust them. Even so, I was not about to give up because I firmly believed that marriage was a possibility for my life.

I am always amazed at how much our lives must change from our former selves once we have surrendered to the Lord. God is never interested in our greatness in the eyes of the world, but He is interested in our humility, faithfulness, and obedience to His Word. I was busy trying to figure out what to do next and all the time it was written down for me in the Bible. The Bible that Pastor Wayne had given to me sat on a book shelf for almost four years. No one discipled me or told me to keep going to church in order to transform and renew my mind to the will of God. I was trying to figure it all out by myself (just as I always did) and I wasn't even getting close. I did however, have a tremendous advantage over my previous life; I knew in my heart that I was saved and that I could call on the name of Jesus.

In late September of 1992, four years later, I still had not found a church home. I had not prayed or spent very much time, if any, with the Lord. I was under tremendous pressure in my personal life. I was angry to the point of rage almost all the time because of circumstances that I thought were beyond my control. The year before, my mother had passed away. I was very close to my mother, yes, I was a mama's boy all my life. I joined the Navy, my way of running away from home, to prove that I was not a mama's boy. I know that I was in and out of many relationships with women to show them that I did not need or want a woman telling me what to do and prove to them that I was a man. (Actually, I was only a male.)

Additionally, I had transferred to Washington D.C. from Hawaii the previous year. I was separated from my second wife for over two years, and I knew that we would never get back together because I believed too much damage had been done. My military career was under attack with threats of a Courts Martial or an Admiral's Mast. I was deep in debt with a drinking and a gambling addiction and I was tired, dejected, depressed, and extremely angry all the time. I just wanted everything to just go away. I had requested retirement in January of that year, and I was just weeks away from the final day of my active duty. The only good thing that was in my life was a wonderful woman I had met just two months before. I even knew that I wanted to marry her, but I believed that I had to get my life in order first.

When life reaches its darkest point, that's when light, any light shines the brightest. I was facing the most frustrating depressing time in my entire life. I felt that there was no one who could do anything to stop the madness. I had been seriously contemplating suicide for over a month. I was spending far too much time alone at home drinking or sitting in dark movie theaters crying, hoping that no one would notice. I had lost my appetite for real food. If it wasn't for the popcorn and beer nuts at the bars in the neighborhood, I would have starved to death.

I had been thinking about making the upcoming weekend my final one on Earth. It was Saturday morning and I got up earlier than usual. I had a plan. I was going to write a bad check for $1,500.00 and then go to Atlantic City. I thought if I won big, then I would be okay, but if I lost, that would be the final thing I would need to justify taking my life. I got dressed and then looked up the nearest location of an American Express office. I was going to use my AE card to write the bad check. I found one that was a few miles away and drove there. I went in and there was a line of about eight people. As I stood in line, I began to think about what would happen if they found out that my check was no good and called the police and had me arrested. That would really mess up my plans. I began to panic. I began to get sick to my stomach. Just as I was next in line, I left the office. I went back to my apartment and I began to drink.

I was home alone on that Saturday and evening was fast approaching. I had been drinking and depression was closing in on all sides. I felt the pressure of everything that I had ever done wrong and I knew that there was no way to make it right again. My only thoughts were on how to take my life and on how to hurt as many people as possible. I wanted everyone to feel the pain and suffering that I was going through. I wanted everyone who had a part in my suffering to pay for what they had done to me. I wanted to let everyone know what they did, so they would be held accountable for my death. If only I could think of a way to do all of that, I wouldn't hesitate to get it over with. However, one person kept coming into my thoughts and I could not get rid of him. I didn't want to hurt everybody, no, not my sisters and brother, or my son and daughter. I thought that the lady that I had just met would understand. But one person kept blocking everything that I was planning and that person was my father, my dad.

During the past two years, I had been through a number of life-changing courses that had truly helped to open my eyes to the life I was living. I had heard many men and women curse their fathers and talk of unthinkable things that their fathers had done to them. I always felt embarrassed to tell them about the wonderful father God had blessed me with. He was always there for me and my brother and sisters. He was a teacher and listener and a doer. He was then and is today one of the most respected men in our hometown of Gary, Indiana. I knew that I could always count on him and all I had to do was ask. I wanted to hurt a lot of people that night, but I just could not find a way of taking my life without hurting my dad.

I always felt like I was a failure to my dad. If he was ever hurt or embarrassed by my divorces or by my being locked in jail for a night at twenty years old for underage drinking, or by anything I ever did or said, he never let me know it. My, how much I wished I could have been half the man and father that he was. I have never met anyone to this day that I admired more or respected more. Yes, I have told him this in private and in public. God gave him to me as a father, so that I would have a glimpse of the Dad that He was for me just because I loved His Son, Jesus. And all I had to do is obey His commands.

That night in 1992, I saw a glimmer of light that God shone into the blackness of my bedroom. That glimmer of light was love. It was in the person of my father, but it was love all the same. I called out to Jesus that night for help and He answered. Jesus got me through the night. Even though I did not sleep, I can't remember those final hours. They seemed to pass in a flash.

The next thing I knew, it was morning. I got up and staggered into the living room of my apartment. I turned on my TV and would you believe it, there was someone preaching on a Christian channel. I didn't know there was a Christian channel; it was Pastor Frederick

K.C. Price. I got mad all over again. I thought that all he wanted was money, so I sat down to watch and see how much he would ask for. He never asked for any money that morning, but he did begin to talk about the Bible and things that I did not know were even in the Bible. I remembered that I had a Bible from four years ago. I got up and looked for it and there it was, right on my bookshelf. I got it down and began to follow along, as best I could. As the program was about to end, I found myself begging Pastor Price not to go off the air.

Of course, the program ended and I was left with my Bible in my hand. I began to read the New Testament that week in order to be prepared for Pastor Price next Sunday. I did this virtually every week for a year. I even sent my offerings to his ministry. I was so blessed by his ministry on that Sunday morning that it was three and a half years later before I ever remembered that suicidal Saturday night again. I never had another thought or memory of planning suicide for three and a half years. It wasn't until someone was talking about suicide at the church where I had become a member that I remembered that dreadful night. Praise the Lord! When you call on the name of Jesus, He is quick to answer and quick to heal.

So you may be asking what did all of that have to do with marriage and relationships? It has to do with the transformation that I had to go through in order to be used by the Lord to minister on marriage. I had been counseling individuals and couples since 1979 on a variety of topics. I had all of the Navy's training for drug alcohol and substance abuse, race relations, and career counseling. I had hours of study in counseling in my degree program. However, I had no idea how to counsel anyone until I found out what the Word of God had to say on the subject. I was embarrassed to tell anyone that I had been married twice before, and yet I was counseling them on their marriage. I thank pastors Steve and Tina Gunn, now ministering in Pasadena, California, for believing in me and my wife, for training and using us in their marriage ministry. This is just a part of the transformation that God required on my part, and I know that there is certainly more to come.

As I continue to share in this book, I want you to know that this book is from my personal experiences, from things that I gleaned from books, tapes, and conferences, but it is mostly from the revelation that I have received from the Holy Spirit. I thank God for those whom God brought across my path to impart into my life. I especially thank my Lord for not giving up on me and for empowering me to do this work for this day and time. God's hand was certainly on my life long before I surrendered my life to Him.

The Lord told me back in early 1993 that He could not use me in ministry until I was married. I knew this in my heart. I did get married for the third and final time in May of 1993, to the lady who stood by me in my darkest hours. This time I am doing it God's way by following His Word on marriage. It is over twelve years later and it has been and is glorious. Yes, we have our own problems, but they are nothing when we apply the Word of God. God must be an integral part of your life and your marriage. I promise you, if you allow God's Word on marriage to be the foundation of your marriage, you will overcome any and all attacks against your marriage. You will have the most joyful, fulfilling relationship with your spouse than you ever dreamed possible. Trust in the Lord and in His Word. He truly will never leave you or forsake you.

The Lord, God is always there for you. His hand is right there on your shoulder right now. Don't wait until the last moment to call on Him. Remember, you have an adversary and he will try to stop you. He does not have the power to stop you, but that won't stop him from trying to deceive you or trick you. Don't give up no matter what comes your way. God can turn it around late in the midnight hour, but don't put your life in danger to prove, just believe it. Just call upon the name of Jesus and He'll take it from there.

Husbands Love Your Wives

"Husbands, love your wives, just as Christ also loved the church and gave Himself for her, that He might sanctify and cleanse her with the washing of water by the word..."
"not having spot or wrinkle or any such thing, but that she should be holy and without blemish." Ephesians 5:25-27

The Word of God is the foundation for your marriage, but the love of the husband is the pillar. Husbands love your wives is a command from the Lord. I know that "wives, submit to your own husbands" is stated first, but it also goes on to say, "as Christ loves the Church." Jesus loved the Church before the Church submitted to Him. The wife's submission is a result of the unconditional love a husband has for his wife. If you do not love your wife, she will never submit to you. I counsel many couples and I hear it said often that "my wife will not submit to me." My reply is "because you do not love her enough." I know that was not what they wanted to hear, but it is true. The success of the marriage is up to the husband for the most part. I have to add "for the most part" because your wife does have free will, as we have covered in the previous chapters. God will not interfere with anyone's free will, including your spouse. However, God's Word does say and command husbands to "love your wife," therefore your love will overcome her resistance to submit. That is, if she <u>wants</u> to be married.

How does a husband love his wife unconditionally? There is no set rule or guide to follow. The only way to love your wife unconditionally is for her to teach you how. Throw out all of the theories, movies, and especially the soap operas, etc. The blueprint for unconditionally loving the woman you married is always in the making. It doesn't exist for her yet and just when you think you have got it all figured out, she will add to it or take away from it. **Unconditional love is a dynamic process of building an intimate relationship with your wife.** (This may help: Intimacy is NOT sex—Let me say that again; Intimacy is NOT sex.) Let me add this to help <u>confuse</u> the matter a little more; your spouse does not know what unconditional love is either. How many women do you know who have been loved unconditionally in their lives? I would guess not very many. However, women do know when they are being loved, especially when it is unconditional love. You are just going to have to trust her and adjust to her over and over again. I'll go into more detail in chapter seven, the chapter on love.

God has only one rule for all Christian marriages and that rule is the **<u>#1 Key</u>** to a successful Christian marriage: ***<u>Do not be unequally</u>***

yoked together with unbelievers" (II Corinthians 6:14). This is not a suggestion, but a Command from God. I don't care how many times single Christians hear this scripture, they will still insist on dating and eventually marrying an unbeliever. They will tell you how much they love each other or that God told them that this is the one. I guess that God must forget His Word from time to time. Don't pay any attention to II Corinthians 6:14, God did not mean it. Of course He did! The Bible says that the battle is the Lord's, but the battles you will go through because of your disobedience will not be the Lord's.

There won't be any victories for your marriage until you both are saved, repentant (disobedience to God's Command is a sin), and walking right with the Lord. **There are no shortcuts.** The Word of God was written for the benefit of everyone who is willing to obey it. So, please don't start out your marriage in disobedience to the Lord. You will call on Him often and He will <u>NOT</u> hear you. Galatians 6:7 says, ***"Do not be deceived, God is not mocked; for whatever a man sows, that he will also reap."*** <u>Do not mock God!</u>

Now, after you are married, after you have both vowed to each other, then the rule for your marriage is <u>husband, love your wife</u>. It is also vitally necessary on the part of the wife to receive her husband's love. Again, trust is going to be a major issue, especially if your have been hurt in a prior relationship. Being loved unconditionally will be new and unexplored ground for both of you. Walk down that path of love together. Be ready to give in and never to take from each other. It will take time, a lifetime, to explore all the avenues of your love, so be patient and let the Lord Jesus show you the way.

Being vulnerable is also a mandatory part of unconditional love and it is not so easy to do. Vulnerability is not something you can turn on and off whenever you feel like it. Vulnerability is a position of strength and self-confidence. I know people think about it as a weakness because it opens them up to being hurt (actually expecting to be hurt). It is quite the opposite. The expectation of being hurt will guarantee that hurt comes. Using the excuse that you were only being vulnerable as the reason for being hurt is a falsehood. No one allows themselves to be vulnerable unless they know that they are safe. You cannot be weak or insecure and be vulnerable at the same time. All of your guards will be up and in place. Avoiding another hurtful relationship will be your daily goal. Being vulnerable won't even be a possibility for you. Vulnerability will allow you to open up your heart in order to give and receive love. Fear is not a factor in the presence of a vulnerable heart.

There is a saying that goes like this, "whatever you run from you run to." Whatever you are afraid of will come to pass. You will spend your life thinking so much about the thing you are trying to avoid that you will create it. Trying to avoid another bad relationship will surely create it. Until you have regained your self-confidence, DO NOT get involved in another relationship. Please, at all costs, do not marry someone on the "rebound."

If you are hurt, weak and insecure, then that is what you bring to the relationship. Anything that is built on weakness and insecurity cannot stand for very long. Anyone can be strengthened or edified by another person (in a counseling or supportive role), but not in a physical relationship. You will not be there for them. The relationship will be about you and all of your problems. It may feeeeeel nice initially, but you will become a burden and a yoke around their neck. You will be in the relationship to take and not give. So, pursue healing first. Get your life in order and then you will be in the right position to find someone to love, and you will be able to give them love.

Also, if a woman finds a man who works hard at loving her unconditionally, yet she is insecure and weak, she will not be able to receive his love. He will be frustrated and it won't be long before he finds another woman who wants his love and he will be gone. Love can be given away, but it is not always received.

Husbands, love your wives is God's command to the man, but it is the responsibility of the wife to receive his love. Having said that, please don't give up if you are a frustrated husband who truly loves his wife and there seems to be a minimal response from her. How you love her is important. I am not talking about sex. I am talking about the things that you call love and the things that mean love to you; do they equate as love to your spouse? If she has been telling you she does not like the things you say or do and you are waiting for her to "get used to them," then you are way off track. If she says she doesn't like roses and you keep on giving her roses because you read (or worse, the woman in your previous relationship loved roses) she will eventually come around, stop it. Listen to her, even if you don't think she means it. Love her as she desires to be loved. She will teach you how to love her unconditionally.

The love you have for your wife will be measured by what you do and not only by what you say. (People will know you by what you say, but they will define you by what you do.) As a husband, the head of the household, it is your assignment from God to take care of your wife and children. It is not an option. I Timothy 5:8 says, ***"But if anyone does not provide for his own, and especially for those of his household, he has denied the faith and is worse than an unbeliever."*** In other words, you cannot abandon your wife and children for any reason, including serving the Lord. His Word says you are an unbeliever and unbelievers are not called into the fivefold ministry by the Lord to preach His Gospel. Your love is real when it is spoken, if it coincides with what you do. Your unconditional love for your spouse will be measured by what you **do**.

You should expect to see your love for each other grow as the time passes. The things that you thought your spouse needed to change will eventually disappear from your mind as your love grows for them. You know the things that I am talking about. When you met, maybe they were only a seven or an eight on your scale of ten for the perfect mate. You couldn't find a ten, so you settled for a seven or eight. After a few years, the two or three things that they did not have to make them your ten begin to become the focus of the marriage or relationship. The next thing you find is someone with the two or three things that your spouse does not have. Of course, this new person is only a two or three, but you don't notice because they have what you are looking for today. Later you'll find that this relationship won't work either because they don't have seven or eight of the important attributes you wanted in a marriage. The grass may look greener on the other side, but once you're over there, you'll find out, it is just artificial turf.

There is no perfect ten except in your mind. No one can live up to perfection, including you. If you truly love your spouse, then you will see, with time, that those two or three attributes that you had to have to be happy in a marriage will disappear. Actually, you will find that they have more than those ten things you required. That's when you will notice that love does conquer all. Love will remove every spot or blemish. When you look through the eyes of unconditional love, you will see that your spouse is perfect without blemish. You can then see in your spouse what you could not see in yourself. They will become your mirror, a reflection of who you really are. They will help you love yourself.

In reality, it is impossible to love someone else without first loving yourself. **Your relationship with your spouse is one of the bridges that you cross to find the love of God in your own life.** God's love is poured into your heart, but you cannot see it until it is reflected back to you from the one you love unconditionally. Just how much do you love yourself? If you really want to know, then see how much you truly love your spouse.

"So husbands ought to love their own wives
as their own bodies; he who loves his wife
loves himself." Ephesians 5:28

You Are in Covenant with Your Spouse

The Bible tells us that a man will find a wife, not a woman will find a husband. Ladies, stop looking for a good man to marry and let him find you. God has an order for everything because *"He does everything decently and in order,"* (I Corinthians 14:40). Try following God's order. The real joy of marriage is in the getting to know each other through learning to communicate openly and often. Marriage is dynamic. Every day, there is something more to learn about each other. Don't allow yourself to think that you KNOW the other person or have finally figured them out. You cannot figure out yourself, how can you figure out anyone else?

I am amazed at how many people say that their spouse is not the same person they married years ago. I have to reply "you're kidding." Are you the same person years later? NO! How then do you expect your spouse to be the same? People do change physically and spiritually, but not very much mentally without a good reason. That is why Romans 12:2 tells you to transform and renew your mind. You must do it because God will not do it for you. If the expectations that you had for your spouse have not changed, then you are in for a rude awakening. You have been left behind in the past. That's why you're so lonely because you live there by yourself.

Thank God that your spouse is not the same as he or she was ten, fifteen, or twenty years later. Who is he or she now and more importantly, who are you? Don't look in the mirror to find out who you are. You must ask someone else to give you feedback on who you are now. You can read in your Bible to see who God says you are, but even God's Word is hard to accept when it comes to describing you, because it does not match up with your own beliefs. The best person to ask is your spouse. Yes, the one who you think is still the same or has not changed. He or she can give you feedback also, but like the Word of God, you won't be able to accept it from them either until you get out of the past. You are the problem and your spouse has the answer.

What did you bring to the marriage? Did you marry to get or to give? Are you a giver or a taker? Is your spouse your partner or a hired hand? If your marriage is all about what you want, need, and desire, then you are a taker. You are an all-consuming fire and your fuel supplier will eventually give out. Turn things around and see your spouse as you would want to be seen. Love your spouse as you would want to be loved. Stop following the world's rules on marriage and relationships. The secular world is always self-focused because it is in survival. Christians are not of the world, but are only in the world. It will take the Word of God to transform and renew your mind, if and only if you allow it to enter your heart.

Most people are looking for someone to fulfill their dreams and/or someone to give them what they want, and to be responsible for their happiness. If you are one of those people, I have some bad news for you: That person does not exist. You are responsible for your life and everything that happens in it. As a matter of fact, **your life is exactly the way you want it to be right now.** You got yourself to this point with the decisions you've made, the words you've spoken, and the actions you've taken throughout your life, that is, after the age of reason. If you continue to make the same decisions, speak the same words, and act the same way, then do not expect to have anything different happen in your life.

I think it is good news to know that you are responsible for your entire life. If you got yourself into the situations that you are in today, then you can get yourself out of them. However, if someone else is responsible for your life, then you have to wait for them to come around and get you out of the situations that you don't want to be in anymore. Stop blaming each other for what is wrong and being prideful about what is right.

Do you remember your marriage was a free will choice established by a spoken vow? You vowed first to each other (horizontally) and then to God (vertically). Honor your vows. ***"What God has joined together let not man separate"*** (Matthew 19:6). That scripture includes the husband and the wife. If you both are in pursuit of unconditional love, then how can your marriage possibly fail? If you are only in the marriage for what you can get out of it for yourself, then how can your marriage possibly succeed? Remember to place your spouse first and let no one (human or thing) come before your spouse for any reason.

Ephesians 5:28 tells husbands to love their wives as they love their own bodies. This is where the pillar of your marriage should stand. Yet, many people enter into marriage after first agreeing to what is called a prenuptial agreement. Where is love found in a marriage based on a prenuptial agreement? Just think about it; you first find a lawyer to draft an agreement that spells out the terms of the DIVORCE before you have married. Planning the divorce before the marriage guarantees that the divorce is going to happen. The person with all of the material assets (assets that he or she want to protect from their future spouse) is trying to make their position perfectly clear. This person wants their future spouse to know that material possessions will always be more important. Their real desire is for material possessions, not a husband or wife. If their future spouse ever tries to come between them and their possessions, then the marriage is over. What a loving arrangement.

People who demand prenuptial agreements are self-seeking people who profess their love in spoken words, but display their aloofness in written words. I believe both partners think that one day they will "really" learn to love each other and then the prenuptial agreement won't matter. Right! That's not going to happen. They are not vowing to a marriage, they are vowing to a divorce. They are simply attempting to make their "shacking up" legal in everyone's eyes. It may be legal in the eyes of man, but it is not lawful in the eyes of God.

God fully expects every Christian to keep the vows of marriage that they have spoken into existence. God has never taken vows lightly, when they are spoken in accordance with His Word. You can make vows for many things, but if they are not in accordance with God's Word, then they are just words. There are people who take vows of poverty; in the sight of God, that is not a vow. His Word says that poverty is a curse. If you want to bring a curse on yourself, then God will not stop you, but you are certainly not held to that type of vow by God. If you make a vow in marriage to someone of the same sex, not only is the vow meaningless, but the marriage is also meaningless in the eyes of God. Whatever the vow may be, be sure that you fully understand what you are doing. Vows are for life, so don't make them lightly. In the Book of Ecclesiastes 5:2, 4-5 it says, *"Do not be rash with our mouth, and let not your heart utter anything hastily before God..." "When you make a vow to God, do not delay to pay it; for He has no pleasure in fools. Pay what you have vowed – Better not to vow than to vow and not pay."*

Restoration of the Marriage Covenant

The Bible says, in the beginning God created them male and female and called them Adam because He saw them as one flesh. After they both <u>sinned</u>, God no longer saw them as one flesh. They

67

had broken their relationship with Him. God's relationship with mankind would not be restored until His Son, Jesus, restored it some 6,000 years later.

Let me stop here and bring up a point that will be important later on. <u>Technically</u>, Adam and Eve were not charged with sin in the Garden of Eden. They did disobey God's direct command and for their disobedience, death was assigned to them. Death was the consequence of their disobedience. They died spiritually in that moment of sin and they would die physically in the future. However, sin is not charged to mankind until God defines sin to Moses in the Ten Commandments and in His Laws. The Apostle Paul states it precisely in Romans 5:13, ***"For until the law sin was in the world, but sin is not imputed [charged; blamed; or credited] to mankind when there is no law..."*** Sin always, always, always has consequences. Repentance intervenes and stops the consequences from being fulfilled. Repentance can also stop the consequences from reaching their full force once they have started.

The consequence of sin is death, in the spirit immediately and of the flesh eventually. <u>Evil is exalted in sin because sinning is a choice.</u> However, <u>evil is glorified in iniquity</u> because it can be passed down to other members of a family and show up in their lives without their prior knowledge. Addictions are examples of iniquity passed down. In the cities of Sodom and Gomorrah, in the land of Canaan, evil was everywhere and the iniquity of the father (Ham, the father of Canaan) was manifesting in homosexuality, yet sin had not been imputed because Moses had not received the Law from the Lord to pass on to mankind. The Law would not arrive for another two thousand years. Yet, their evil ways and iniquity brought forth death by the devastating consequences of fire and brimstone rained from heaven.

I included this point of sin because of the "spiritual warfare" that exists in the world, but is ignored and denied even by Christians. The attacks against marriages and relationships within the Body of Christ are primarily satanic and demonic with one purpose, and that is to steal, kill, and destroy. I also, brought up this point because of the conversation that says that Eve did not sin, but Adam did. Now, you know neither sinned (technically) but death is always the cohort of evil, iniquity, and sin.)

Additionally, sin does have levels of magnitude. Adam had the greater sin because he directly disobeyed God's Command. He was in direct rebellion against the Command of God. Eve, on the other hand, was truly deceived. Because Eve was deceived by the devil, God's punishment for the devil included the promise of Eve's "Seed" coming to destroy him one day. God did not say the seed of Adam, but the "Seed" of Eve or woman (who is Jesus Christ). The consequences of the devil's sin included retribution by or through the woman. Everyone reaps what they sow, including the devil.

The life, death, and resurrection of Jesus Christ restored God's Covenant with all of mankind. God sent His only begotten Son, Jesus, to remove the wall of separation between mankind and God. The New Testament or New Covenant is God's Word, His bond and it is for all time. As a Christian, you have the right to speak your vows to God and establish a threefold bond with the spouse of your choice and with the Holy Spirit of God. God once again looks on you and your spouse as one flesh.

In the Old Testament, the covenant was between God and His people, the Israelites. Their marriages reflected this covenant by men having many wives. However, that was never God's plan for marriage. In the New Testament, the covenant is between God and each person as an individual. God literally has NO grandchildren. Each individual enters into a one-on-one relationship with the Lord. There is no need for a priest or prophet to stand before the Lord on your behalf. You can speak directly to the Father in the name of His Son, Jesus.

In marriage the covenant is the same; it is between God and both spouses as "one flesh." Just as God called Adam and both Adam and Eve came to heed His call, when God calls those who have vowed in marriage, He speaks to them both as the Smiths, Joneses, Adamses, etc., and also as individuals. It is God's intention for the wife to have the last name of her husband. He is the head of the household and God's blessings flow through him for the entire family. It is the world's way to encourage the woman to maintain her identity.

(It is the women's liberation deception and the Baby Boomer self-centered agenda.) If you want to remain individuals, then do not expect God's blessings for marriage. Remove all forms of division from your marriage. (That is what keeping your hyphenated names does, it maintains division in the marriage.) Do it God's way or do it you own way, but be fully aware of what you are doing.

(Please do not be offended by what I have written. I am simply pointing out some things that I believe will help you receive the full blessing of God for your marriage. I know that this is not how the world does things, but that is exactly why God wants it that way. You are in the world, but you are not of the world.)

Jesus has fully restored marriage as a covenant in the eyes of His Father. Therefore, enter marriage as a covenant with the Lord. Fully expect God to hold up His end of the covenant; He will not break His Word. And God fully expects you to uphold your end of the covenant to remain married to the same person and love each other as He loves you. God will provide the love that He gives for each person. God will provide the victories and even fight the battles on your behalf. All you have to do is stand on His Word and have faith that He will do what He says. What a great deal!

In the eyes of God marriage is forever. God will not change His mind about marriage or divorce. Did you know that God hates divorce, (Malachi 2:16), whether it is between a man and a woman or between a nation (Israel) and Himself. God made man in His image and likeness. He made woman from man, bone of his bone and flesh of his flesh so that they would always be one with each other and with Him.

> *"For we are members of His body, of His flesh*
> *and of His bones. For this reason a man shall*
> *leave his father and mother and be joined to*
> *his wife, and the two shall become*
> *one flesh." Ephesians 5:30-31*

There is so much wisdom contained in the above scripture for married couples. This scripture helps to clarify one of the two most recognized areas of conflict in a marriage: the spouse's family and money. We will talk about money later.

Pitfalls of Marriage

How many married couples do you think have problems dealing with their parents, siblings, and in-laws? Practically every married couple that have family members have some sort of conflict on going with their families. I have seen so many couples set free by Ephesians 5:30-31, *[31] "For this reason a man shall leave his father and mother and be joined to his wife, and the two shall become one flesh."*

God knew that these conflicts would occur and that is why He had an answer ready. It is a delicate subject with most couples because of the influence that mothers, fathers, sisters, and brothers have on marriages. Your family members have known you all your life and they believe they know what is good for you and who is good for you. It doesn't matter how old you are. It doesn't matter if you live a thousand miles away; those family members will want to control your married life. I know this is a sensitive matter, but it must be dealt with.

The Bible says to leave your father and mother. It does not say to disrespect them, but it does say to leave them. It does not mean to leave them physically, although that may be necessary. It means to <u>leave them out</u> of your marriage. Your father and mother cannot come first in your life anymore. I know that they have known you longer than your spouse, but that does not matter. It is not about who knew you longer, but it is about who you have vowed to love. As I said earlier, love is action or doing, not just words. Your family will not allow you to love your spouse unconditionally because they don't want their relationship with you to change. They want to help you love your spouse, the right way, on their terms. They know you and so they know you don't know what you are really doing. They believe you need their counsel and guidance. So, they constantly put pressure on you to include them in your marriage relationship. Of course, this can be a continuous source of strife for you and your spouse.

At this point, you may be feeling trapped with no hope of escape. You may be living with your parents and they have daily influence on your marriage. If so, just refer them to Ephesians 5:30-31 and move on with your new life. If they cannot agree with the Word of God on this matter, then start preparing to find another place to live. Don't be held hostage by your family because of money. It is not easy, but it is necessary. Remember, I am only speaking about Christian marriages.

The husband, as head of the household, is responsible for taking care of his family. Unfortunately, it is usually the husband's mother who is the problem. He must speak up and not let his wife be blamed or attacked by his family members. Your wife comes first, before all of your family members. She even comes before the children at all times. Ephesians 5:30-13 is not just addressing parents, but anyone who comes in between you and your spouse. If a family member refuses to accept your spouse, then let them know, in no uncertain terms, that they are not welcome in your home and that you can no longer have a personal relationship with them. This especially goes for your best friend or friends. They all must go if they attempt to come between you and your spouse. Remember, you are in a vowed relationship with your spouse and not with any one of them. They may mean well, but good intentions don't always bring good results. If you are serious about your marriage, then you must act in accordance with the Word of God.

God has reestablished His role in relationship with mankind and you must obey His commands. You must keep Jesus in your marriage. The only way to do that is to read your Bible daily. Read it with your spouse as often as you can and be a member (not a visitor) of a local church. Do you pray together daily? Do you spend time with each other without the children, family, or friends? Jesus wants to spend time with both of you individually and together. God sees you as one flesh. He created you to worship and serve Him together as one. When He called Adam, both he and Eve answered. When God calls to you, do both you and your spouse answer? Do you have a private relationship with God that does not include your spouse? God wants a personal relationship with each of us. However, He does not have a private relationship with an individual that does not include their spouse. Your spouse is not just along for the ride with you and God. You may not necessarily be doing the same task, but the assignment must include you both. God honors marriage. Marriage is always your first ministry assignment.

Remember, the fivefold ministry is a calling from God to an individual. The calling does NOT come from another person. It can be acknowledged by another person through ordination and the laying on of hands. You can refuse the calling if you choose, and it is not a sin. However, marriage is a vowed relationship. Once the vow is made, you cannot walk away from it without sinning. You may change congregations in your calling, but you cannot change spouses in your marriage vows. Also, you cannot return the children that God blessed you with in the marriage. Recognize that your marriage always comes before your calling. It is and will always be your first ministry.

Sin and Forgiveness

Isn't it amazing how much you can feeeeeel that you "love" someone and then after a period of time you can feeeeeel that same "love" for someone else? The five senses send messages to your brain to let it know what is out there. The five senses are pleasure seekers and pain sensors. You are not your five senses, but you have five senses. You are not your feelings, but you have feelings. You are not your emotions, but you have emotions. This may sound elementary, but I can assure you that many people don't get it. Because their lives are based on how they feel or whatever the emotional dilemma they're going through that day. People like this have totally lost touch with the reality of the present. They seek to be loved, but love no one. Their conversation is all about the pain, suffering, and hurt that they are enduring because of other people. They cannot forgive anyone because they refuse to be accountable or responsible for anything that they did. Their lives are based on the past and how to change it or fix it. Life is passing them by and they are not aware of it.

As I have already said, love has nothing to do with how you feel. Feelings can become the excuse or justification for **sin**. Saying, "I no longer love you, therefore, I am attracted to someone else" is just an excuse for **sin**. There is NO justification for **sin** in the eyes of God. *"He has delivered us from the power of darkness [the devil]..."* (Colossians 1:13). That is why you must repent for **sins**, not make excuses for them.

If a situation arises in which you are attracted to someone else, then tell your spouse and pray together about it. (I know it's not likely that you will tell each other.) However, if you do not take authority over this attraction, it may lead to adultery. Adultery is a symptom of a bad marriage. Adultery is a **sin**, not an excuse. At least one of the following two conditions must exist before adultery can occur. The first is the husband does not love his wife, and the other is the wife is not submitted to her husband. If either of these conditions exist in your marriage, then please recognize that you are in position for a fatal attack against your marriage. That attack is called divorce.

Do not be deceived, any and all sexual acts outside of marriage are **sins**. I think that when sexual **sin** is discussed, the emphasis is often on homosexuality, but any sexual act outside of marriage is a **sin**. Let's be clear, there isn't a place in hell that is a little cooler for the adulterer or the fornicator, than for the person committing the sin of homosexuality. God says that the **sin** of homosexuality is perverse and abominable in His sight, but that does not make adultery or fornication less of a **sin**.

(I hope that as you are reading these pages, you don't get the impression that I am saying that our feelings and emotions don't count. As a human being, you do have feelings and emotions that have a tremendous impact on your life. Because you are human, you cannot ignore how you feel, but you must, at the same time, not let those feelings and emotions take control over your life. There is no justification for sin and that includes adultery and fornication.)

Why is adultery so hard to forgive? Adultery is betrayal. It is an extremely serious betrayal in the relationship of marriage. You vowed, gave your word, and now you have broken it. You are no longer one flesh with you spouse, but you have now established a "soul tie" (fleshly relationship) with another person. They can now freely occupy your mind as well as entice your soul. Your relationship with God is BROKEN! Your relationship with your spouse is BROKEN! You need to repent to the Lord and ask forgiveness from your spouse on unconditional terms. <u>You are in full-blown sin</u>. Your life is at stake because death has surely been assigned to you.

In the book of Genesis, chapters 11 and 12, King David lays out for you the consequences of adultery (and murder) and the role the Lord has in bringing "healing" to both his and Bathsheba's life. King David had an adulterous relationship with Bathsheba and she became pregnant. Because of this he had her husband, Uriah, murdered in battle. Later Bathsheba gave birth to a son. (Remember, when you sin, death is assigned to you.) David repented and the prophet Nathan told him, ***"The Lord also has put away your sin, and you shall not <u>die</u>. However, because by this deed you have given great occasion to the enemies of the Lord to blaspheme, the child also who is born to you shall surely <u>die</u>"*** (II Samuel 12:13-14).

God never touched King David, but the consequences for all of King David's sins led to the death of many people. However, when King David repented to the Lord, the Lord forgave him and cast his sins into the "Sea of Forgetfulness." After King David repented, God allowed him to marry Bathsheba and gave them another son and they named him Solomon. Of course, Solomon became king and continued the lineage right up to the birth of Jesus.

When you repent of your sins, God hears and He is **"faithful and just to forgive us our sins and cleanse us from all unrighteousness."** (I John 1:9) Repentance is a right of believers. You must speak it in order for God to act on your repentance. God is an ever-present God; He will hear you and forgive you. In His presence, all things are possible.

God forgives in the present. When you come before Him and repent, He hears you and is faithful to forgive you. There was no remembrance of King David's sins. It should be the same with God's children. If you are truly a Christian, then you must pursue forgiveness. I know how difficult it is to forgive unfaithfulness through adultery. I am always amazed at brothers and sisters in Christ who are quick to

75

forgive, even adultery. They truly love their spouses, themselves, and God. They have chosen to forgive rather than carry around their hurt and disappointment. This is no small thing for a person to do, but if you do as the Bible tells you to do and give your cares over to Jesus, then you will be able to forgive. You must stay in the present and not continue to relive the past, dwelling on the event. You cannot forgive anyone while reliving the past offense and focusing on their sin.

In the book of Matthew 19:8, Jesus tells the Pharisees that divorce was allowed in adultery because of the "hardness of their hearts." He did not say that they could get a divorce because of the adultery, but because of the "hardness of their hearts." Jesus recognized that your heart will become hard and even cold after you have been hurt or betrayed by the adultery of your spouse. He said that because adultery breaks the vow to both your spouse and to God. Your word is no longer valid and therefore it invalidates your vow that was established in your declaration to Him. Instead of trying to get your spouse to forgive you, first repent to the Lord. Declare your word to Him in repentance and then approach your spouse. It is never God's will to have anyone (Christians) divorce.

God's Word will soften your heart. God will heal your heart for your spouse. You must have faith that He can and you must be willing to forgive, unconditionally. The adulterous event is in the past and it cannot be undone, but it can be forgiven. You must get into the present because the event is not happening to you now, in the present. It is not happening to you in the future, so don't create it with talk of it happening again. Don't let fear be the reason or excuse for you to look into the future and see it happening again. Don't let your mouth speak of it occurring again, while you allow your heart to heal. It may still take some time for your heart to heal. Spend your time with the Lord, telling Him how you feel and trust Him by your faith to heal your heart. God healed King David and Bathsheba and poured His love back into their hearts. God will certainly do the same for you.

God will certainly heal your heart, but He will use people to help you heal. You must find someone in the church that you can talk to about the event. The more you talk about it the faster you will heal. Do not let it be a secret buried in your heart. Expose it to the light of fellowship and watch it transform from a victim story into a testimony. A marriage that has overcome adultery is a powerful testimony to the Body of Christ. *Confess your trespasses to one another, and pray for one another that you may be healed. The effective, fervent prayer of a righteous man avails much.* (James 5:16)

If you are a Christian and your spouse is a Christian, then you have found the right person in the eyes of God. There is no one else that God has for you. Your marriage is real, it is not a fantasy or a dream, so stop dreaming of someone else who will make you happy, or fulfill your needs, because that person does not exist in the flesh. Jesus is the only person who can and will fulfill ALL of your needs. He'll even give you the desires of your heart, when they align with the Word of God. Be ready to fight for your marriage. Be prepared to stand on the Word of God, so that you don't fall for the lies of the devil. Your marriage will be under spiritual warfare attacks, but they are just attacks; you have to surrender to them in order to lose. You made a commitment to be married and you declared your vows. Now, stand on your word.

Your marriage is more than a commitment. A commitment is something that is stated and then completed. Your marriage is more than a completed commitment. It is a declaration. A declaration establishes whatever it is you say. Once it is established, it can withstand any storm that may come against it. However, it can only stand against the storms that you choose to take authority over. Also, once your declaration is established, only you can destroy it.

If you decide to give up on your marriage and file for a divorce, then please don't blame your spouse for that. They did what they did, but you quit on the marriage. Be responsible for your own actions, because once the enemy knows your frailty, he will visit you again. You will live in fear of the same thing happening the next time with someone else. You will be so cautious that you will imagine it (adultery) even if it doesn't happen. It may happen that it's you who commits the sin of adultery the next time because you cannot stop dwelling on it. Let go and let God take over. Jesus is the answer! The Book of Job 22:28 says, *"You will declare a thing and it will be established for you."* You declared your marriage. It is established in heaven in the eye of God. God will honor your vows just as long as you honor them. He will forgive you just as long as you are willing to repent. Trust in God! God is good all the time.

The Reality of Relationships

"You shall love the Lord your God with all your heart, with all your soul, and with all your mind…" "You shall love your neighbor as yourself" Matthew 22:37-39

God is seeking a personal relationship with you every day. I don't know how many times that needs to be said, but it did not sink into my belief system for years. As I learned to love my wife unconditionally, I discovered that I also learned to love God unconditionally. I began to see Him as Father and began to talk to Him as Daddy. Jesus is my Lord and Savior and He is also my brother; through Him I walk in righteousness. God desires for all of His children to come closer to Him every day. The hurdle is our love, not His. I believe that God gave us our parents, spouses, and children to see how much we were willing to love them. Love must be practiced. It must be defined by those to whom we freely give it.

How do you love yourself? It is impossible to love yourself in isolation. Mankind was created to fellowship with each other. There are even people who say that they are Christians and say that they don't like people. There may be some people you do not like to be with, but there should be no one that you don't love. I heard Brother Jesse Duplantis say that "Jesus did not like the Pharisees, but He loved them enough to die for them." There will always be people who do things that we do not like, but do not confuse that with God's command to love them. If you love them, then you would want them to be saved. It is God's desire that all be saved, and it must be your desire also.

The issue comes down to how do we love anyone, including ourselves? If I am commanded to love my neighbor as I love myself, and I don't love my neighbor, then it is only a reflection of my lack of love for myself. It is impossible to love someone else until I first love myself. God reveals the hardness in your heart in order to heal it. He brings people across your path so that they can reflect how you truly feel about yourself. The hate you may have for someone is a reflection of the hate you have for something in your own life. I say this because hate is not from God. Nowhere in the Bible does it say that God placed hate in your heart. If it is in your heart, then it is from the devil. It is a choice to hate another person. That choice is against the Word of God. The person you hate is yourself because you are cutting off your communication and relationship with God. You are the ultimate loser where hate is concerned.

God knew you would not be able to love yourself just because He told you to. Love is reflected and revealed by your relationship with another person. Other people teach you how to love yourself. Your neighbor will teach you to love yourself and no neighbor will ever be closer to you than your spouse. What does your love for your spouse look like—silence, loneliness, hitting? What does it sound like—yelling, cursing, or swearing? If so, why are you so angry at yourself?

If you say that your spouse is the reason for your anger, then are you saying you were never angry before you met your spouse? You brought anger into the relationship from previous relationships. You've found out that anger gets you something, something that you want, attention, respect (perverted), your way. In reality, anger only gets you separation from God. If you allow anger to grow into wrath, then you are in sin, and death is very near to you. Don't ever try to manage anger. Anger is spiritual and your flesh cannot control it. Take all of the courses that you want and anger will still be there. Read all the books on the subject and do all of the exercises that say they help to define anger; but at the end of the day, you will have less control over anger than when you started. You cannot manage spiritual things, but you can take authority over them in the name of Jesus.

I have been teaching the concept of taking authority over anger for over fifteen years. This is not just a concept, but God's way of dealing with anger. I have counseled hundreds of people about anger. I have seen many of those hundreds take authority over anger and find peace. Speak to anger, but don't call it yours. It does not belong to you, it belongs to the devil. You can command it to go from you, in the name of Jesus. Don't let it become a yell, something you punch, or something you throw. Each time you give anger an identity, you reinforce its presence and power. Command it to go and always in the name of Jesus. The name of Jesus has the power to send anger fleeing away from you. It may come back, so be ready to do it again and again and again. Learn by practicing to keep your mouth shut and your hands to yourself when you feel anger approaching. Speak to it with authority and see what happens. Of course, I am talking to Christians, those who have Jesus as their Lord and Savior. Demonic forces do not respond to non-believers, but obey the authority of a believer. Don't play around with anger. Take authority over anger immediately in the name of Jesus.

Take authority over your relationships by taking authority over your life. <u>The reality of relationships is that they rise and fall with your ability to love, to be loved, to forgive, to leave the past in the past, and to live in the present.</u> Proverbs 3:5-6 says, *"**Trust in the LORD with all your heart and lean not on your own understanding; ⁶in all your ways acknowledge Him, and He shall direct your paths."***

Remember, God is an ever present God. He will see you through every trial, test, and tribulation that comes against you.

Abuse Is a Choice

"Let each one of you in particular so <u>love</u> his
own wife as himself, and let the wife see that
she <u>respects</u> her husband." Ephesians 5:33

As I near the conclusion of this section of chapter four, I have to address another area that rears its ugly head in far too many marriages. That is violence between spouses. The vast majority of spousal abuse cases involve husbands attacking their wives. I have known counselors (pastors, lay leaders, and even Christian professional counselors) who tell the physically abused spouse to just pray for their husbands and let God heal him. I also believe that

God will heal him because God is the only person who can heal him. However, God will probably need a little help from the abused spouse in this area. The best way you can help God is (are you ready to hear it) to call the police and put him in jail. File charges and don't back down. If he physically abuses your children, please, please, please call the police and put him in jail for as long as possible. It is amazing how a little concrete authority (jail cell or prison) can help in the healing process. I want you to know that you are putting your life in danger and your children's lives in danger anytime you tolerate even one incident of physical abuse. He has vowed to love you, and love does not have violence in it!

I have seen many physically abused women allow their spouses to return, in spite of a restraining order, Temporary Restraining Order (TRO), and have him severely injure them. God's command to husbands is to love their wives, not harm their wives. If that is his definition of love, then there is no marriage, because he is a liar and his vows are meaningless. Let me say it one more time: Do not play around with an abuser. He abuses you only because you allow him to do it. Stop enabling him to abuse you and not get the help he needs. I know there are incidents of wives physically abusing their husbands, and they should be treated the same, especially if their children are being abused also. I have counseled a few of these couples too. They don't get reported because of the embarrassment of the situation. Men don't want to admit to being abused by a woman. However, some women can be just as dangerous. Put them in jail, it is the Christian thing to do.

People who physically abuse other people are also fighting for their lives in a spiritual warfare battle. They need prayer and lots of it. They also need restraint while they are dealing with these attacks. They are not necessarily demonic, but they can be. Let the police get involved as an impetus to their accepting counseling and receiving their healing. Sometimes it is necessary to get their attention first before they will accept counseling. Afterward, do not allow them back into your life UNLESS they have joined (and are a member) a Christian church and they are faithful in their attendance. Be careful; you do not want to go to the same church with them. If they show up at your church, inform the pastor. If there is a Temporary Restraining Order (T.R.O.) still in effect, then have them arrested. If it is later, but you are not back together, then you both may want to begin counseling with the pastor or church lay counselor, <u>individually at first</u>, and then together. Take your time in the restoration. If children are involved, then take a lot of time. Don't let anyone tell you that you are not being Christian. You are absolutely being a faithful Christian. God is our Father and He does not want His children to be abused.

There is no abuse in love. There is no out-of-control anger or violence in love. Love is kind, not weak, but kind. Work on your relationship with the Lord, Jesus Christ. Jesus will change your heart and drive out all of the wrong thinking and ungodly behavior from your life. The love of God never fails.

Now let's talk about personal healing and restoration. I know from experience that an abused person doesn't want to hear that they are an integral part of the abuse. You may have a belief in your mind that says that you deserve the abuse. It is always difficult to get a physically abused woman to act on her own behalf. She will deny the abuse for as long as she can. Even when it is apparent, she will make excuses for her husband, or others. I can guarantee you that the abuse did not start with the spouse. The abuse started with low self-worth. It is a result of believing that you are less than or not enough in comparison to other people. It doesn't matter where these beliefs started. It matters that you act on them in the present. All healing takes place in the present. I know that there are some counselors who want to go back in the past to find out what happened, but even if you know what happened, you still have to deal with it now, in the present. You cannot change the past, alter or relive it. If you will come into the present, you will find out that God is there. God is always in the present. He is waiting for you to show up and receive from Him.

Believing God's Word is simple. It is the application of His Word by faith that's the hard part. You are not going to figure out how God heals, and you don't have to. God heals and all He requires of you is to have faith for your healing. If you are living your life with your eyes on the past, then there is no present or future. You cannot get to the future from the past; you must stop for that nanosecond of the present and demonstrate your faith with words or action. If you keep looking in the past, you will keep repeating your failures. The answers are not in the past, but they are in the present.

(If you were standing by a swimming pool and someone you did not see set your clothes on fire, what would you do? Would you look around and try to find out who did it, while you are burning up? Would you just jump into the water and put the fire out? If you found out who did it, would that put the fire out? In the present, the fire is the ISSUE, not who did it. If you are in the present, then putting out the fire is your first choice and the only choice under the circumstances. I know there must be someone who is thinking, what if I can't swim? I guess now you really have a dilemma. Do you burn or do you jump in the water?)

I know this all sounds like it should be a "no brainer," but most people are spending their lives trying to figure out how their lives got so messed up, instead of living in the present. I'll say it again, even if you find out why and how you screwed up your life, that information will not change your circumstances. Information or knowledge about your past is just that, knowledge. Leave the past in the past and live your life in the present where your decisions and choices can make a difference. Of course, I am not talking unresolved issues of the past. Until these issues are resolved, they will not go away. Unsolved issues are not past issues, but present issues.

In the world's system information about your past is vital for your treatment. However, in God's system it is immaterial for your healing. The choice is yours. If you do not learn to use your faith, then your choice is to be treated. Understand that it is okay to be treated, but it is not God's best for your life.

In the Gospel of John 5:6-8, Jesus asks a sick man *"Do you want to be made well."* The sick man began to tell Jesus all about his circumstances (the past). He was focused on the reasons for his sickness and not on his healing. Jesus said to him right in the middle of his victim story, *"Rise, take up your bed and walk."* I know it is hard to believe that the circumstances of the past don't matter, but it is true. The circumstances will always get in the way of your healing.

You must get into the present and stay there. You cannot get to the future from the past.

The point of all of this is who is responsible for the things that are happening in your life? Your life is exactly the way you want it to be right now (if you are past the age of reason). I know that this is not what some of you want to hear because it means that you can no longer blame other people for your life's problems. You cannot look back and pinpoint an incident from your past and use it as an excuse or the reason for your present condition. I know this goes against the prevailing world view, but so does being born-again, the resurrection of Jesus Christ, and the rapture of His church. That's okay because you are not of the world.

I have some more great news. You can actually do something to make permanent changes in your life so that you do not have to repeat the past. It is called transforming and renewing your mind. The Word of God can transform you and it can renew your mind. You will have to surrender the beliefs that got you into all of your troubles. The Bible calls that process in Philippians 2:12, working out your own salvation. If you want to continue to believe you are not worthy or you deserve what life is dishing out for you because of some obscure event from your past life, go right ahead. You have the right to exercise your free will and God will not stop you.

Speak what the Word of God says and stop speaking what you believe and watch the power of the Lord change your life. Love God and be quick to forgive. You may still have the scars of the past to remind you that you were hurt or abused. Just remind yourself that the scars are wounds that have healed. The only way to feel the pain that caused the wounds is to open them up again. Don't reopen the wounds of your heart. Stay in the present where wounds are healed and remembering the pain is a choice.

Four Stages of Relationships (Marriage)

In this final part of chapter four, I want to be sure that you have a clear understanding of relationships and how they apply to marriage. There are basically four stages of relationships. You have probably seen them expressed in different forms and styles, but I like to use the following stages because of their simplicity. The four stages are honeymoon, conflict, communication, and growth.

The Honeymoon Stage

This is the first stage of a relationship. It is not just about marriage, because it can be applied to any relationship. In the honeymoon stage, when two people meet, everything is just great. You meet someone who could possibly meet all of your needs and fulfill all of your requirements for a lasting relationship. Although they may have faults, you are willing to overlook them because you are blinded by infatuation. Even when their faults are glaring, you are willing to make excuses for them because you know that they will change as they get to <u>know you better</u>.

The honeymoon stage is great because the focus is on them, not on you. Yes, you are conscious of how you look and behave, but your real focus is on what you expect from them. As long as the honeymoon lasts, you will refuse to deal with any real issues that may arise between the two of you. If trusted friends or family begin to tell you anything about this person that you don't agree with, you are quick to ignore them or avoid them in the future. This is the one and no one is going to spoil it for you. Enjoy this stage, because it will not last forever, thank God.

The Conflict Stage

In this stage, reality begins to set in. You both have made your commitments to each other; now you just want things to continue on as they have been. Then, without warning, you wake up and realize that this person of your dreams doesn't want to live there (in your dreams) anymore. They have faults and scars and moles and bad habits and many other little things that you didn't quite notice before. Of course, you don't want to say anything about those things, yet, because you still believe that they will go away as they get to know you better.

As I mentioned before, this person was a seven or an eight on your scale of ten. Now, the two or three missing attributes are beginning to show. You discover that you don't want to spend every single moment with them now that you can. You need some space, some borders, and some more time to figure out what is happening. I'll tell you what's happening: <u>You have begun to see yourself in them</u>. All of the things that you don't like in them are really the things that you don't like in yourself. Whenever you look at them, you see a reflection of yourself. You are beginning to discover that the dream person that you have been trying to find really is just a dream. You may begin to think that if you had just held out a little longer, you would have found the right one. You'll give them a try for a while and see what happens, but they had better begin to show some progress before too long. You don't want to be embarrassed by getting out of the relationship too soon and have all of your family and friends be right about them. Maybe they will change and become exactly what you expect them to be. In the meantime, you'll just continue to pray about it.

For many people, this is as far as their relationship will ever go. Somewhere in the conflict stage, they will give up and quit. They won't see any solutions because they have already figured this person out. They couldn't possibly love you because they are always fighting with you. They won't even apologize when they are wrong or even worse, acknowledge that you are right. You have already decided that counseling would not help, because there is a chance that the counselor might say that you are at fault. You can't have that happen. So, the conflicts rage on and on, until the only real solution is a D I V O R C E. It is surely a good thing that you paid that lawyer all that money to draw up that prenuptial agreement. That was smart on your part. You just knew somewhere deep in your soul, that they would not work out, and by golly, you were right.

You may begin to think that you somehow missed God on this one. You know that God really has someone for you. Next time, you will be more cautious and diligent in your search. You might take some courses or read a few more books on marriage and relationships before you begin to look for someone else. The next person will have to show you how much they really love you and prove it to you. You'll listen a little more carefully to God and make sure it's His choice for you.

The Communication Stage

What does it mean to communicate? It means to talk, to speak, to connect, to be in touch with another person. Did it ever occur to you that while you were spending so much time in the conflict stage, that talking about the problems just might help? Of course not; they should know how you feel and even what you are thinking, if they really loved you. They should have learned your sign language or what is so popular today, your love language by now. Why talk or even attempt to communicate with them when you can just observe them or read a book about them and finally figure out who they are? After all, you can be one step ahead of them all the time because now you'll KNOW them. Now that you have completed your studies on how to figure people out, you are ready for that next relationship. What you're really preparing to do is repeat the past.

The communication stage is where you get to know each other, not the honeymoon stage. **The honeymoon stage is for your mind-soul, but the communication stage is for your heart-spirit.** You have to begin to put self-centered interests behind you. You have to be willing to be wrong. (I know it is easier to get a divorce than to admit you're wrong, dead wrong. I've been there and I've got the T-shirts.) The communication stage is where you begin to build the character, integrity, and humility you'll need to be successful in your relationship. You don't enter a relationship with these characteristics. Yes, you may have them all as an individual, but they don't count for a relationship with another person until you are actually in a committed relationship. Your values change, your habits will change, and your foundational beliefs about men and women will have to change also. You have entered the rebuilding zone, where transformation and renewing your mind are required.

The communication stage isn't a one-stop event. No, you must be willing to reenter this stage often. It is the place of healing from the conflict stage. As long as you are both different people, you will have conflicts. No two people are alike, and trying to find a perfect match based on the things that are compatible is ludicrous. Your lives will be constantly changing all the time and you both must be willing to make adjustments as the need arises.

However, as you visit this stage, you will find that it will get easier and easier to resolve your conflicts. It will get easier to surrender your pride and self-righteousness for the sake of love. You will notice that you are learning to be your word. Showing up in the present will provide all the excitement and joy needed for your relationship to last and prosper. You can only enter the communication stage in the present. You must leave the conflict stage of the past, travel through the atmosphere of truth, burning up pride, arrogance, and fear, and land in the fertile valley of communication. If you're successful, you'll find yourself on the peak of the mountain of growth.

The Growth Stage

The fourth and final stage is growth. Nothing grows successfully without first being rooted. It takes time to grow roots. Far too many relationships look good on the surface, but they lack the roots to sustain themselves. How long do you want your relationship to last? That will depend on how much time you are willing to grow your roots. It is not easy to change your beliefs and not get your way after years of doing just that. It is necessary to make changes, not all at once, but over time. Everything has a season to grow and a season to rest, including people. The fruits of the growth stage are almost indescribable. Growth brings seasons of joy and peace and love in abundance as you get to know each other in an atmosphere of love and mutual respect. Maybe you cannot imagine how it would be in a relationship in which you didn't scream, curse, fight, and say things you wish never came forth from your mouth. A relationship in which you were not apologizing all the time for saying and doing things that you should not have. This is what the growth stage will produce.

How often is your relationship in the growth stage? After each conflict, there should be a time to talk about it and as you talk about it, the opportunity to grow in your relationship will be there. There is no limit to how much a relationship can grow. The comfort and peace of being in a permanent relationship is worth every effort to resolve conflicts. Let all of the energy of your emotions subside before you speak to each other. Hold hands and be quiet. Touching brings you into the present and leaves the past behind. Don't speak, just focus on the touch and on the other person. Stop all thoughts of the incident as they try to become words. Be quiet! Touching is communicating. Let the moment pass from the emotional to the sublime. Learn how to express your thoughts in words based on your experience, which is feedback, and not on how your spouse makes you feel or how your spouse is responsible for your feelings.

It will take genuine love for each other to stop blaming and accusing. You have that love within you, so use it. Allow yourself to grow into the person you were created to be and not who you want to be. Your growth is dependent on the feedback (their experience of you in words) you receive from others. Your walls must come down and you must let someone else in before you can grow. Speak from your heart at the moment you are the most vulnerable, because it will be the most powerful time to speak. As I said before, vulnerability is a place of strength. It is a sign of your growth when you are willing to be vulnerable. Remember, you cannot be vulnerable and afraid at the same time. Vulnerability comes when your heart is open. Keep growing and see how much you change as the years pass by.

The Apostle Peter was vulnerable at the moment he stepped out of the boat onto the stormy sea. He had his eyes and attention on Jesus and not on the circumstances. As long as he looked to Jesus he was fine, but when he focused on the circumstances he sank. So, do not let your mind lose its focus on the moment. Let your heart lead the way and listen to it. Your mind will be screaming, you better be careful, you're going to get hurt, watch out! But if your heart is at peace, then follow it. Stay in the present. Remember, running from fear will always lead to you back to your past.

I think it is interesting to see how much our relationship with Jesus falls along these exact lines of the stages of relationships. The excitement and often euphoria that accompanies the honeymoon stage with Jesus is much like the honeymoon stage in your marriage.

Like the joy and all the emotions you felt when you first received Jesus as your Lord and Savior. How quickly that stage changed as your beliefs were challenged by the uncompromising Word of God.

Most conflicts will begin with the sin that you enjoyed so much and now must be surrendered and repented of. That wasn't so easy the first time, especially when it involved another person that you were living with. You want to be saved and in relationship with Jesus, but what about the person you've been with all these years? Does Jesus understand that you love this person and you don't want to lose them? Yes, He does understand. Jesus understands that you are living in sin and He has something tremendously better for you. That's where your faith comes in and why the communication stage is so important in your walk with the Lord, Jesus.

The communication stage with Jesus requires reading His Word. It also requires church membership and to be an active member. It requires repentance of your sins and to avoid committing them again. It is a two-way communication. God has even written down everything you need to know about Him. You can even question Him and pray to Him for understanding and revelation knowledge to help you. As you pursue your communication, you will find that you are becoming stronger and better able to communicate with Him. Before you know it, you will see the growth that you have made in your walk with the Lord. You will notice that you are not the same as you were in the beginning of your relationship. You may have to end some old relationships, but there will be plenty of new relationships available in the Body of Christ. You cannot stay the same in your relationship with Jesus, and He will not allow you to stay the same in your relationship with your spouse.

God is seeking a personal relationship with you. You will go through the stages, but you won't regret it. God is patient. He will wait for you to catch up to Him. He will even help you identify your gifts, talents and skills. He will help you discover who you are. He will bring other people into your life to love you and accept you. He will put His love into your heart so that you can share it with anyone you choose. God is the establisher of relationships. Trust Him to help you establish your relationship with the one you vowed to love. He will never leave you or forsake you. And best of all, He will send the Holy Spirit to walk with you hand in hand all the way through to the end.

Marriage and relationships must be healthy within the Body of Christ. Far too often, they are taken for granted because of church members' involvement in ministries. They think that if they are in a ministry, then God will take care of their families and keep the love flowing in their marriages. If you neglect your marriage, then you will open it to possible fatal attacks by the enemy. God will fight your battles, but only if you are willing to address them first.

As I said earlier, your marriage is your first ministry. There must be ongoing teaching, seminars, and workshops for married couples. The health of the entire church organization is dependent on the condition of the church families. There must also be ongoing teaching, seminars, and workshops for singles. You cannot maintain anything that you take for granted. The attacks will surely come against you, your marriage, and your relationships, so do not help them along by being overly involved in church ministries or church business.

Marriages in Ministry

Church ministries provide opportunities for "members" to be directly involved in church growth. Some ministries are vital and others are nice to have. All of them perform one very important function, and that is to help each member develop in their God-given gifts, talents, and skills. The marriage ministry is vital for healthy church growth. The foundation of the church is built around healthy families. These vowed relationships set the stage for all other relationships within the church body. Family members should be involved in all aspects of church ministries. Using married couples to head many of church ministries will add stability and experience to any church organization.

Church ministries help members to identify their calling. They also provide opportunities for people to see and hear what is on the hearts of others. Character is revealed and integrity is established within these ministries. Often, this is where the strongest relationships are formed and the strongest support for the vision of the church is found. Take every issue that arises in these ministries seriously. They will reveal the areas that require the most attention in the church body. Address personal issues directly, because problems never resolve themselves. Deal with them like any family issue; get everyone involved. Resolve problems face to face with both parties present.

Especially, keep a close eye on one ministry in particular and that is the praise and worship team. Few spouses are both on the praise and worship team. Individuality is more of the focus and not personal relationships. Personal relationships are too often clicks. Most members are on the praise and worship team because of their natural talent, not because of their walk with the Lord. More often than not, they bring their unresolved problems with them and these problems are often involvement with sin. Do not compromise with sin, no matter how much talent they may have. Always put the person first and not their talent. Provide opportunities for socializing, so that they can be observed away from the ministry. Leadership should be involved in their personal lives as much as possible. As their leader, you must know them individually and what their personal relationship with the Lord is all about.

Sin and sin issues enter the church every time a new person attends the church. They are there to be delivered from their sins. However, sin can proliferate in a church within its ministries. Sin proliferates when it is hidden, unfortunately, when it is finally exposed, tremendous damage may have already been done to the members involved and to the church. Again, inspect them often and hold everyone involved accountable for their personal lives as well as their role in ministry. By maintaining a family setting throughout, problems can be exposed early and issues resolved before they become major conflicts.

I am including churches with the cell ministry or a cell church. So that I am not misunderstood, I am recommending that these churches have a marriage ministry in place. If marriages are not addressed directly and problems arise, as they surely will, the consequences can be devastating. Most couples did not marry in the church that they are attending today. So, as pastors, you need to know what they know about marriage, being fathers, being mothers, and being godly parents to their children. These issues must be addressed even in a cell church.

God commands the Body of Christ to be in right relationship with Him and with each other. The church is commissioned by God to carry out His commands. Be aggressive and take the initiative to be a church that stands for marriage and a builder of Christ-like relationships within the entire church congregation. The church will be as healthy as its ministries, and its ministries as healthy as the families that participate in them. Let God's blessing and anointed power for the marriage relationship touch every ministry within the church body.

Praise the Lord!

***

CHAPTER FIVE
FAMILY

"Children, obey your parents in the Lord, for this is right.
²Honor your father and mother, which is the first
commandment with promise:
³that it may be well with you and you may live long on the Earth.
⁴And you, fathers, do not provoke your children to wrath, but
bring them up in the training and admonition of the Lord."
<u>(Ephesians 6:1-4)</u>

God loves family. When He sent His only Son, Jesus, to the Earth, He sent Him to a family. Jesus had a family while He was on the Earth. He had a father and a mother, Joseph and Mary. Of course, Mary was a virgin before she conceived Jesus, by the Holy Spirit (Luke 1): *"…the angel Gabriel was sent by God to a city of Galilee named Nazareth, to a virgin betrothed to man whose name was Joseph, of the house of David. The virgin's name was Mary"* (verses 26-27): *"And behold, you will conceive in your womb and bring forth a Son, and shall call His name Jesus"* (verse 31) *"The <u>Holy Spirit</u> will <u>come upon you</u>, and the power of the Highest will overshadow you; therefore, also, that Holy One who is to be born will be called the Son of God."* (Luke 1:35)

God loves children and He gives them to families. (The husband and wife are the family and they are blessed with children) God also blessed Joseph and Mary with other children (Matthew 13:55): *"Is this not the carpenter's son? Is not His mother called Mary? And His <u>brothers</u> James, Joses, Simon, and Judas? And His <u>sisters</u>, are they not all with us?"* Yes, Jesus had half-brothers and -sisters. Mary was a virgin for His birth only, but she and Joseph had at least six other children. Jesus was not alone as He grew up. He had a childhood like many of you. God does love family and children.

The head of the family is the father. In the Old Testament, God did not have much emphasis on fatherhood. Most of the Patriarchs and prominent men of the Old Testament were not very good fathers. Isaac favored Jacob over Esau. Jacob favored Joseph and Benjamin over his other the sons. King David's father, Jesse, would have left him out in the fields to tend his sheep if Samuel the Prophet had not been sent by God to anoint him king. Maybe it was because of

David's ruddy complexion (a redhead). Even Eli the Prophet had corrupt sons according to I Samuel 2:12. King David's sons were undisciplined and ruthless. I believe that fatherhood was not an issue with God until the birth of His Son, Jesus.

With the birth of Jesus, God's compassion for mankind returned. His Dispensation of Peace was announced, by an angel with a multitude of the heavenly host, to the shepherds in the fields, *"Glory to God in the highest, and on Earth peace, goodwill toward men!"* (Luke 2:14). God's peace and mercy are available to all of mankind. In the Old Testament, God's mercy was presented as the destruction of the human enemy that was fighting against His Chosen People (thanks, Pastor Richard Prasad). In the New Testament, God's mercy is presented as the destruction of the demonic enemy that always attacks His Children. God sent Jesus to do just that, *"the Son of God was manifested, that He might destroy the works of the devil"* (I John 3:8). God was now involved as a Father to Jesus and a Father to all those who believe in Him. Fatherhood is now the focus of God for the Body of Christ.

One of the best ways to destroy a society is to destroy the fathers, or remove them from the household. If you want to control those whom you have enslaved, then remove the husbands from their wives and fathers from their children. Without the head of household's presence, the family is open to attack and certain defeat. In World War II, Hitler used that very tactic. He counterfeited the concept of fatherhood to the German people. He called Germany the "Fatherland." I say "the concept" because he was supposed to be their father figure. He was able to turn the children against their parents because they saw him as the head or father figure of their country. However, he used the power of fatherhood to destroy family values and the lives of millions of people. Just like Satan, Hitler was a liar and a counterfeiter of God's will for mankind.

Families will fight and die alongside their father without hesitation, but they will not fight or die without the leadership of a father figure as the head of their household. Someone must take or assume the father's role in order to bring families together for a common purpose. Hitler was fully in partnership with demonic forces, if not with Satan himself. He taught children to hate their parents, thereby costing them their lives, as it is written in Ephesians 6:2-3: *"**Honor your father and mother, which is the first commandment with <u>promise</u>: ³that it may <u>be well with you</u> and you may <u>live long</u> on the Earth.**"*

Fatherhood

Fatherhood is vital part of the Body of Christ. God has already set the man (not the male) as the head of the wife and head of the family. It is not a topic for debate, but a command from God to be obeyed. Satan has deployed many forces against the establishment of family. He has and is using women's rights organizations to fight against the establishment of God-ordained families. By turning women against family, marriage, and childbearing, he is carrying out his plan to destroy humanity. Satan hates family and he will do everything in his limited power to eliminate family values from society.

There is no question that females have been abused and misused by males, actually since the fall of Adam and Eve from the grace of God. Males have left their wives and children on their own without a care or second thought for their well-being. This should not be a surprise to anyone. It is only fulfilling the punishment of Eve in the Garden of Eden. God said that Eve's desire would be for her husband and he would rule over her. Her desire would no longer be for God, but for man. Man's rule over woman would always be to her harm. It is through childbearing that woman was restored, *"¹⁴And Adam was not deceived, but the woman being deceived, fell into transgression. ¹⁵Nevertheless she will be saved in childbearing if they continue in faith, love, and holiness, with self-control."* I (Timothy 2:14-15) The childbearing that saved woman was the birth of Jesus, who restored woman as a man's helpmate and not his servant or slave.

Fatherhood must be reestablished as a cornerstone within the Body of Christ. Jesus loves His Father and He has invited the church to do the same. He has sent the Holy Spirit to empower and restore the Church to its rightful place. The Holy Spirit is restoring men to their place as head of household, as fathers, and as leaders. This was and is God's plan today. Do not be tricked by any deceitful scheme or movement of the devil in the world today.

God's Word is clear: *"A son honors his father, and a servant his master. If then I am the Father, where is My honor? And if I am a Master where is MY reverence?"* (Malachi 1:6). The church body honors and reverences God through its obedience and faithfulness. Fathers in the Body of Christ must first repent, transform, and renew their minds, collectively, in order to be in right standing with the Lord. They must take leadership roles within the Body of Christ. Then the Holy Spirit will be able to fully establish God's plan for fatherhood, family, and righteousness within His Church.

Attack on Womanhood

"For you are all sons of God through faith in Christ Jesus. 28 There is neither Jew nor Greek, there is neither slave nor free, there is neither <u>male nor female</u>; for you are all one in Christ Jesus. 29 And if you are Christ's, then you are Abraham's seed, and heirs according to the promise." (Galatians 3:26, 28-29) Jesus restored women to their rightful place in the Body of Christ. She is an "heir" and a son of the seed of Abraham just like men, in the eyes of God. She is no longer ruled by man and her desire is for God once again. However, the devil will continue to steal, kill, and destroy where women are concerned. He will continue to attack, but he will not win.

The enemy is not going to stand by and just watch, as the Body of Christ pursues God's righteousness. Expect spiritual warfare to increase, but the enemy will not be any more effective with his tactics. It will disguise itself in many ways. It can appear in organizations that say they are advocates for women's rights, but they are actually demonic forces waging warfare against women and family. For anyone to teach that having children is belittling to a woman is absurd. To teach that being a wife and mother is somehow degrading to womanhood and femininity is absolutely ridiculous. To teach abortion as a woman's right is outright sin. No one has the right to murder another person. For a woman to murder her own child, through abortion, is clearly part of a demonic plan.

Satan deceived Eve in the Garden of Eden and he is deceiving her today through groups and organizations that promote abortion as a means of birth control. God created woman to have children, not to murder them. Satan kills babies, not God. If you do not want to have children, then do not have a sexual relationship. The birth control pill was not made just to stop pregnancy, but more so to encourage sex outside of marriage. Anything that has its root in sin is from the devil. Abortion is murder and no murderer will enter the kingdom of heaven. Abortion is satanic. Why would a woman fight for the right to murder her own baby if it wasn't a deception from Satan?

What about incidents of rape or incest? I believe that each mother, woman, or female must make that decision with the help of her church and family. Let me state this clearly: abortion is a sin! Just because everyone is doing it does not make it right in the eyes of God. I can only imagine (not understand or know) how traumatic it must be for a woman to experience the fear, humiliation, hurt and pain of a sexual attack in the first place; and then to have to make a decision about the unwanted pregnancy that occurred after the attack. Trust God!

Seek godly counsel. If you have enough faith to trust God, know that He will bless the child and you in the future. If you decide to have an abortion, then remember to go before the Lord and repent. God does understand what you are going through because no one knows you better. I am not condoning abortion. If the mother's life is in danger, then the abortion may be justified. I am only giving you the information you may need to make the right decision.

The devil will use other tactics to attack women and destroy their future generations. There are groups that advocate aborting (murdering) your babies so that the pregnancy and/or the baby does not interfere with your lifestyle, your dreams, your vision, or your immoral sexual behavior. These immoral groups encourage your teenagers to be as sexually active as they want to be. If your daughter happens to get pregnant, they will even help her get an abortion and make sure that you, the parent, don't and won't find out anything about it.

Additionally, these groups have the audacity to lobby for laws that give them the right to murder your grandchildren. These groups are demonic in their inception. Of course, everything they do, they do in the name of personal freedom and right to privacy, even when it involves murder. No one has the personal freedom to murder and there is no right to murder babies even if it is done in privacy of their homes or abortion clinics (legalized murder clinics). Legal does not make it right in the eyes of God.

Turning females against males as if they are competing in some superiority contest is diabolical. Using revenge, hatred, anger, and wrath to extract some sort of sick justice for all the suffering that women have gone through at hands of men is demonic in its very nature. The answer is not in revenge for the past, but in forgiveness in the present. Christian women who follow these agendas are being led away from the Lord, on purpose, by the devil. Don't be taken in by any of their programs or theories.

God did not create males to be mothers or females to be fathers. No matter how much psychobabble you may read, neither males nor females are equipped to fulfill each other's roles for their children. God gave mankind the Body of Christ, the Church, to fulfill the roles of the missing parent for families. Feminism, as well as chauvinism, (male superiority) is not from God and it is certainly not a part of anyone's walk with Jesus Christ.

Again, please do not fall for lies and deception of these organizations and groups. The murder of babies, the destruction of family, the perversion of teenage girls and boys, and the elimination of moral values are the true foundational principles of these demonic organizations. Be ready to fight to protect your rights as a woman and as a parent. Stand on the Word of God for your life. It is a God given right to marry, to have as many children as you choose, and to have parental authority over your children. Only Satan, his cohorts, and his followers would want to destroy these rights.

(I'll say one more word on abortion before I move on. Every child that has ever been aborted is in heaven with the Lord. God created them in response to your sexual activity, not in response to your sexual desires. The children who are born from these acts are not illegitimate, not at all, but it's the act of sexual intercourse outside of marriage that is the illegitimacy. To those that say that the fetus is not a human being, I've got news for you, they are living beings, and they have already got a soul, and are therefore human beings. God instills life within the soul immediately at the moment of conception.

Only God can give life. Abortionists hate God! These murders think that they can play God. They must think they have the power to determine who will live and who will die. They must also think how dare God, the Father, the Creator, give a child to a fourteen year old girl, or allow a fourteen year old boy to impregnate a twelve year old girl, or allow females to get pregnant when all they were doing was "enjoying" sex. Who does God think He is to interfere with people's lives by giving them "unwanted" children? If God is really the Creator, then He should have known that these people He created were only having "fun" and had no intention of getting pregnant. What kind of a God would do all of these hurtful things to such innocent people? People that think like that don't know God and certainly don't know Jesus.

Of course the real battle that is raging is a fight for supremacy. God or no God, these murderers are telling God that they are in charge of their own lives. They will determine what they will do with their bodies. If God does not agree, then they will just be atheist and dismiss Him. If God really offends them, then they will join a satanic cult and fight openly against Him. They will steal, kill, and destroy until God gets it and does things their way. They'll murder so many babies until God gives up and lets them live any way they choose. They'll bring God down to their depraved level, right on top of the 40,000,000 babies that they have already murdered, in this Country, the United States of America.

What these murderers will find out, when it is far too late, is every human being created will live for all eternity. The aborted babies (not embryos or fetuses) are in heaven looking down watching and observing you. Where will you be in eternity? Will you be with them in heaven or will they still be looking down from heaven observing you? Given the choice of life or death, choose life. Choose God's way of living. Death is just the door into eternity. When it opens for you, where will you be? The decision is up to you.)

Another attack against womanhood that needs to be addressed is pornography. This demonic plan to use women against women has been a major cause of family breakup. Pornography not only has a devastating affect on wives, but also on the children. I'll give you one example:

- A woman came up to me at church one Sunday and asked me if I could counsel her husband. I'll call her Mary. She said that she was considering getting a divorce because of his "infatuation" with pornography. As she was telling me this, she began to cry. She said that they had not made love to each other in over a year. He never touches her even when they are in bed together. However, that was not the worst of thing that was going on. She said they had three daughters, ages 17, 14 and 12. She said he never spends a moment with any of them and he acts as though he is ashamed of them. All of these things had been going on for years, but had gotten worse over the last two years.

- I told Mary I would certainly talk with her husband as soon as possible. I also told her that her husband had to be willing to be counseled. She said that she would ask him to call me later that afternoon.

- I already knew that there was a problem because her husband, Mike (not his name), had approached me a few times before and told me he wanted to talk to me, but he never did. I saw Mike a few times afterward, but he would always say that he would get back to me.

- Mike did call me that day and we met the following day at lunch. He was visibly shaken because he knew Mary was serious about getting a divorce this time. He did not want to lose his family and the promise, not threat, of a divorce made him realize that he had better get some help. He felt as though he had no control to stop his behavior. He stayed away from Mary because he was ashamed of himself and he did not think she would believe him about being out of control and helpless to stop his behavior.

- Mike had been living in fear of the demonic spirit called pornography. He stayed as far as possible away from his daughters because he did want to take the slightest chance of doing anything wrong or sinful to or with his daughters. He was actually terrified that he might do something wholly inappropriate to one of his daughters.

- Mike's life was a mess because of pornography. I was thankful that he was willing to finally get delivered and healed from this demonic attack. Mike and I met three times that week for approximately two-three hours each time. His progress was immediate. He was quick to understand that he had to take authority over the situation. He did not need treatment, he needed healing. Remember, Jesus is a healer and He has no treatment programs.

- James 5:16 tells us to *"confess your trespasses to one another, and pray for one another, that you may be healed. The effective, fervent prayer of a righteous man avails much."* This is exactly what happened. His confession mixed with fervent prayer laid the foundation for his healing.

- Mike's total healing came when he confessed his trespasses to his wife and also to his daughters. He said he did not think that they knew what he was doing, but I assured him that they did and probably always knew. He gathered up ALL of his pornographic materials and along with his wife and daughters they burned them up. He got to see that season of his life go up in flames.

- Mike and his family destroyed the objects of pornography on Saturday, one week after we first spoke. On Sunday morning, I saw Mike walking toward the church WITH HIS OLDEST

105

DAUGHTER ON HIS RIGHT ARM! Walking right behind them was Mary and the two younger daughters. When she saw me she began to cry (we all did). She said she had her husband back and her daughters had their Dad back. Praise the Lord! God deserves all of the Glory.

- A powerful side note to this testimony is that the daughters will not be involved in a relationship with a male who is also "infatuated" with pornography. Mike's attempt to hide his sin from his daughters only guaranteed that they would one day find a male just like dad. By confessing his sin to his family, he exposed the evil of pornography so that his daughters understood. Now, they would be aware of this danger in their future relationships.

- There is a saying that is so true, "whatever you run from, you run to" because you cannot avoid the thing that has your focus and attention. It is only a matter of time before it overtakes you. You must take authority over it in the name of Jesus. There is no other way around it. Surrender it to the Lord Jesus. Jesus is the Son of God, and He gives to each of you His burden removing, yoke destroying power of God. Amen!

I shared this testimony to show the devastating affect that pornography can have on an individual as well as every member of his family. While pornography is usually a male problem, it is directed against women. Women are deceived once again by the devil into throwing away their self-worth and degrading themselves. They allow themselves to be used to destroy men and their families. Their reward will be a life of chasing worldly fame and fortune only to end up used, abused, and confused, if they're fortunate, if not, dead at an earlier age.

No woman can compete with the demonic spirit of pornography. No man can control the destruction that will surely accompany this type of spiritual warfare. It has the power to steal, kill, and to destroy if you allow it. Without the intervention and help of God all will be lost.

As I have stated many times before, Satan hates women and families. Don't let him have his way with your family. If you are battling with pornography, don't believe that you are defeated, FIGHT BACK! Satan has been defeated by our Lord and Savior, Jesus Christ. Use the power that the Lord has already provided. Just do what the Word of God says to do, please, do not make it hard, or turn God's delivering and healing power into something super spiritual. The Word heals, so use it as God intended.

Jesus is the answer. The problems are issues of the heart, not the head. The answers will come in the spirit in the heart, not in the mind or flesh. If you want to believe in "sexual addictions" then go right ahead, but as I said earlier, there is no such thing. It is not sexual addiction, but sexual sin. Addiction has nothing to do with it. Take authority over your out-of-control sinful sexual practices through the Word of God. Repent and be delivered and healed.

Is the power that God has given to you as His disciples making sense to you yet? I pray that is it.

Follow God's Direction

Fatherhood is God's plan for mankind. Being a faithful husband is not an option. Anyone can father a child, but not just anyone can be a dad to a child. To be a dad, you must be a man, not just a male (it is a choice), however, you must first be a <u>husband</u> to your wife. God will hold you accountable on Judgment Day because it is written in your life's records and you will hear it again on that last day. If you do not want to be a father, then do not engage in an immoral sexual relationship. This is not rocket science. Have you heard people say they just don't know how she got pregnant; or say they cannot believe she is pregnant? She is not pregnant because it was an accident, because the condom broke; or because she forgot to use the pill, or foam, or diaphragm, etc., etc., etc. She got pregnant because she had sexual intercourse with a male. And because it was outside of marriage, it is sin and death has been assigned to her.

107

God has assigned the man to be the head of the household. It is not the woman's responsibility to "protect" herself from becoming pregnant. It is always the man's responsibility in the eyes of God. God gave the man the seed. If he does not provide the seed to the woman, then pregnancy is not possible. As God restores fatherhood within the Body of Christ, He will also restore the male's pursuit for manhood. It is the role of fathers in the Body of Christ to teach the teenage males how to become men. (Little boys do not become men because they have to become teenage boys first.) Teenage boys become men. Teenagers have waited long enough for the men of the church to stand up and fulfill their rightful place. As they do, then the mother will no longer feel the obligation to try to act as a father and teach her son how to be a man (which she cannot do).

Ephesians 6:4 says, *"And you fathers, do not provoke your children to wrath, but bring them up in the training and admonition of the Lord."* It is important to understand the full intention and meaning of this scripture. Do not provoke (aggravate, hassle, irritate, inflame, rouse, whip up, incite, or needle) your children. Hitler did exactly this to the children of Germany, while the fathers stood by and watched. Do not incite them to wrath (rage, fury, or uncontrolled anger). Many fathers do this by their treatment of their wives. If you are abusing your spouse, then watch out, because your children are being incited to wrath by you. However, bring them up in the admonition (caution, warning, reprimand, or approval) of the Lord. Proverbs 22:6 says, *"Train up a child in the way he [she] should go and when he [she] is old he [she] will not depart from it."*

God is telling fathers that He will hold them accountable and responsible for how their children are raised. It does not matter if they are present or not, God will hold them responsible for their children and accountable for their proper raising.

I cannot stress enough how important strong marriages are in the growth of a church. Strong marriages produce strong family values and Christ-like behavior from children, teenagers, and young adults. A father, again, is the catalyst. A husband cannot show more love and affection to his daughter than he does to his wife. This behavior is all too common in the church. He will spend time with his daughter, remember her birthday, see that she has everything she needs and wants, speak to her with respect and admiration, buy her things without her asking, and (without thinking) put her before his wife (who, by the way, is her mother and teacher).

A husband may yell at his wife, but never his daughter. If that is you, you are setting up a potentially dangerous situation. Your daughter, as she gets older, will begin to disrespect her mother and turn to you for answers and companionship that should only come from her mother. She will begin to act out the role of the wife and even try to "protect" her father from her mother. Of course, if the wife is putting down her husband and expressing her unhappiness in front of her daughter, then the situation will only get worse. Do not blame your wife; you set this up by being the ruler of the household and not the head of the household.

I brought the up topic to bless you and not to condemn anyone. I brought it up to make you aware of it. Showing more love for your daughter than for your wife sets your daughter up for a future of failed relationships with both men and women. She might have been Daddy's little girl before the age of reason (nine to twelve years of age), but after that, your relationship with her must change. She must learn how to be a woman from her mother, not from you. A man cannot teach a female to be a woman. He can only teach her what a man wants from a woman. That is why the church must have women who can step in and fulfill the role of motherhood for a family that does not have a mother.

Likewise, a mother cannot show and give more attention to her son than she does to her husband. While he is a child, that is to be expected, but as he approaches the age of reason (ten to thirteen years of age), then you must be conscious of the change and take a step back for the relationship of the son and father to develop. The mother should not be her son's "best friend" and neither should the father be the daughter's "best friend." Just because a teenage boy shows respect for his mother does not mean that he will show respect for teenage girls, and later in his life respect for women. Boys learn respect for girls from the respect that their fathers show to their mothers. Your teenage son will also feel the need to "protect" his mother from his father, especially if he sees and hears his father disrespect her in front of him. Again, the church will have to provide the role model for families without a father's presence.

I am often asked to provide counsel for teenagers who have problems in the home. I don't like to do that. I tell the fathers that the problem is that they do not love their wives enough. They certainly don't want to hear that answer, but the Bible says for husbands to love their wives and not to anger their children. If husbands truly love their wives unconditionally, then most of the problems in the home will be healed.

Teenagers learn to disrespect their parents from watching their parents disrespect each other. Teenagers do what they see and hear, not necessarily what they are told to do. What kind of relationship do you have with your children, both the young and the teenagers? Does it resemble the relationship you have with your spouse? Do they act toward you the way you act toward your spouse? If the answer is yes, then husbands love your wives. The love you have for your wife impacts every relationship you have, especially with your children. Love your wife the way God loves you, unconditionally. It is the role of the church to teach you how to love each other the way the Lord loves His church.

I know that there are many church members who have been married more than once. I have witnessed many second and third marriages suffer and struggle because of false teaching on divorce and remarrying. Many will blame the breakup of a second marriage on the children from the first marriage. This theory is even taught in psychology. However, it is not true. The second marriage may end in divorce, but not because of the children, but because of the spouses' lack of love for each other. Children are an addition to the family, and the family is the husband and wife. If either spouse places their children before their new spouse, then the marriage is in deep trouble. It does not matter how old the children are, they still come after the spouse. You must make that clear from the beginning. Do not tolerate rebellion from the children because of your decision to marry again or for any other reason. Stand on the Word of God. Husbands love your wife, and wives, submit to your husband. Let God guide you from there.

Divorce

I better add a few words on the subject of divorce. Divorce is a sin for reasons that I have shared earlier. Any sin that you are willing to repent to God, He will forgive. Some churches seem to think that divorce is some sort of unpardonable offense to God. What chapter and verse is that written in? Was divorce too big a sin for Jesus to deal with, so that it now remains? I hardly think so. You will not stop being a human being. Even though you are saved, you will still commit sins, from time to time. It is not up to God to prevent you from sinning, it is up to you. If your heart is too hard to forgive offenses committed in your marriage, then you will eventually get a divorce. (Actually, the divorce happened long before you filed the paperwork with the court. It happened when husbands disobeyed God and stopped loving their wives and when wives stopped submitting to their husbands. These were commands, not suggestions from the Lord.) God simply requires repentance for the forgiveness of sins. If God forgives you, then the church certainly ought to forgive you too.

God warns the church that a person will commit adultery if they remarry after a divorce, so that they must <u>repent</u> and get their lives right with Him before they look for someone else to remarry. God forgives completely any and all sins that you are willing to repent to Him. When King David committed adultery with Bathsheba and had her husband, Uriah, murdered by putting him on the front lines in battle, God forgave King David and Bathsheba completely. King David repented before the Lord and God forgave him. He allowed them to marry and then He blessed them with a son, Solomon. God forgave King David and Bathsheba. Remember, God is no respecter of man. God will certainly completely forgive your sins, even divorce.

Never hold back your repentance. Be quick to repent, because there are always at least three witnesses to your sin: you, God, and the devil. It is the devil's death sentence that will eventually catch up to you. Stay in the present and continue to serve the Lord in your calling and in your ministry. Leave your sins in the past, in the Sea of Forgetfulness, where God has placed them.

Rebellion

The Body of Christ must become more aware of the need for teaching their members parenting, child rearing, and classes on fatherhood and motherhood. Children will find their own role models if they are not provided for them. The world would love to be their teacher. If the church does not do something about it, then the world will take every opportunity to turn the hearts of the children away from the Lord Jesus.

The Bible says in John 17:15-19, *"I do not pray that You should take them out of the world, but that You should keep them from the evil one. ¹⁶They are not of the world, just as I am not of the world. ¹⁷Sanctify them by Your truth. Your word is truth. ¹⁸As You sent Me into the world, I also have sent them into the world. ¹⁹And for their sakes I sanctify Myself, that they also may be sanctified by the truth"* and in I John 2:15-16, *¹⁵"Do not love the world or the things in the world. If anyone loves the world, the love of the Father is not in him. ¹⁶For all that is in the world—the lust of the flesh, the lust of the eyes, and the pride of life—is not of the Father but is of the world."* The church must set the standard for our children, so that the world can not easily deceive them. You cannot keep them from the world, but you can teach them to take authority over the things of the world.

Have you noticed the rise in deaths among teenagers and young adults? I can remember when I was growing up that there were only a few funerals for teenagers. There was the occasional teen who had been sick for a long time or maybe some infrequent accident may have claimed the life of some teen that I knew, but for the most part, there were very few. Today, it is a daily occurrence for a teenager to be killed by violence, sickness, or accidents. Parents are far outliving their children. There is a proliferation of senior citizens' homes that are filled with people who have no living children or other living relatives, for that matter.

If people are truly living longer today, then why are there so many early deaths of children? I believe it is clearly stated in the opening scripture, Ephesians 6:2-3, *²"Honor your father and mother, which is the first commandment with promise: ³that it may be well with you and you may live long on the Earth."* Long life and living well are promises from God. This Fifth Commandment is the first commandment with a promise. Every commandment from the Lord also comes with predetermined consequences for disobedience. A short, hard, and difficult life is the consequence for breaking this Fifth Commandment. (Only God's mercy can override His justice for sin.)

In the Old Testament days, there were laws that directly addressed the rebellion that you see in the youth of today. The Word of God in the Book of Deuteronomy chapter 21:18-21 clearly spelled out what parents were to do with stubborn and rebellious children. To paraphrase, the father and mother were to take him to the elders of the city and say to them that he is a stubborn and rebellious son and he will not obey; he is a glutton and a drunkard. Let me give the direct scripture for what they did next in verse 21: *"Then all the men of his city shall stone him to death with stones; so you shall put away the evil from among you, and all Israel shall hear and fear."*

God told them to stone their rebellious children because of the evil that rebellion brings into the family and the congregation. (Of course you do not stone your children today because you have a better Covenant with the Lord in the New Testament. Love is the answer.)

Rebellion is a serious sin and it cannot be tolerated in any family or congregation. In I Samuel 15:23, it says, *"For rebellion is as the sin of witchcraft, and stubbornness is as iniquity and idolatry."* These are serious sins because they declare Satan as your lord and master. You are an idol worshiper and follower of evil. The iniquity from prior generations has taken up residence in your heart. God had a solution for this level of wickedness and that was to destroy the carriers of this wickedness before it spread throughout the entire congregation. During that time, parents loved the Lord more than they loved their children and therefore, obeyed the Lord without hesitation.

113

I Samuel 15:22 says, *"Behold, to obey is better than sacrifice."* God was teaching His Chosen People to love Him unconditionally.

(Let me take a moment to clarify something about the Sixth Commandment, "Thou shalt not kill" because there is so much controversy about this subject. The actual translation is "Thou shalt not <u>murder</u>. Think about it, how could God give His people a commandment not to kill and then tell them to kill all the inhabitants of the Promised Land? They understood the difference, but today many Christians do not. God does not always explain everything that He says or does. It is not important that we understand everything that God says or does, but it is vitally important that we OBEY everything God commands us to do without reservation or hesitation.

The death penalty is not against the Word of God in the Bible. Sin has consequences and ultimate consequence of sin is death. Praise God that males and females that commit horrific crimes sometimes receive their salvation in prison. However, their salvation does not mean that they have transformed or renewed their minds, so that they will never commit their crimes again. There are still consequences and punishment to be fulfilled, and sometimes the price is paid with their lives.)

I hope that you are getting the true picture of what is happening in the homes, families, and churches in America. It is spiritual warfare disguised in social movements. The so-called Baby Boomer generation was created from the spirit of rebellion. They were in rebellion against family values, social order, morality, and most authority. Values like honesty, integrity, character, humility, responsibility, accountability, and keeping your word became meaningless. These human values just got in the way of their pride, selfishness, greed, and fleshly desires. Of course, white collar crime, abortion, and sexual depravity became their lifestyle. Parenting became a bother and their parents became expendable, thus, the proliferation of senior citizen homes. The only things that mattered were how they felt and how much money they could get their hands on, not necessarily earn, but obtain through any means necessary.

Today, the sinfulness of the Baby Boomer lifestyle is catching up to them. There are more prescription drugs to take, more medical specialists to see, more sickness and diseases than ever before. There are more doctors and hospitals, and yet hospitals are overcrowded and understaffed. People are sicker, disease is proliferating and all the while people are taking more and more prescription drugs—that do not work. Over five times the number of people die from the side affects of taking prescription drugs than, the 50,000 plus that die in car accidents.

I believe all of these things are a result of the sin of rebellion. The seeds of rebellion have produced a harvest of moral decay and early death. *"For the wages of sin is death, but the gift of God is eternal life in Christ Jesus our Lord"* (Romans 6:23). The only way to break the cycle of spiritual warfare of rebellion is through turning to God, repentance, and in some cases, restitution.

Christianity is not of the world. Christianity has the answer to all of the world's problems and the answer is Jesus Christ. God's Word is not only a command, but a warning to those who are perishing. *"Honor thy father and mother"* is a command and most certainly a warning for today's society.

The Jezebel Spirit

This is good place to discuss another rebellious spirit that targets women, marriages and relationships and churches. Actually it is as much a leadership issue as it is a marriage or relationship issue. I don't know how to present this in a delicate manner, so I'll just present it. This demonic plot is called the Jezebel spirit.

Since the fall of Adam and Eve and the prophecy of the coming of the "Seed" of the woman, Satan has had a burning hatred for women. This attack is directed against women, but it also includes the church, its congregation, and its leadership.

Jezebel was the wife of King Ahab. She was the daughter of the king of Sidon. Sidonians were people that were not driven out the Promised Land, as they were supposed to be, by the tribe of Asher. They worshipped Baal (one of Satan's disguises), a god of immorality. Since they were allowed to remain in the Promised Land, their pagan gods and immoral lifestyle became a part of the lifestyle of the people of Israel. Jezebel began rule as if she were king and the people were afraid of her. King Ahab was a coward, and he was afraid of her and refused to correct or stop her from committing all sorts of sins against the God of Israel, Jehovah. (Read 1Kings chapters 16 through 22.)

In the church setting people often talk about some woman with the Jezebel spirit attacking their pastor or causing other problems within the church body. There will always be bold strong willed women in every church and there should be. There are even rebellious women in every church. However, the real problem is weak leadership from the church leaders. Unless the pastor is as weak as King Ahab, the Jezebel spirit will not cause widespread destruction throughout the church. Pastors and church leaders who will not tolerate this behavior eliminate the threat before it can become a problem. That's why I said it is a leadership problem.

The woman with the Jezebel spirit does not show up in church by accident. She was sent to your church because of the opportunities already in place for her rebellion to succeed. Weak leadership will always be targeted for attack. This is true in life, families, business, organizations, military, and of course in the church. Being afraid of this spirit will only encourage its presence. You cannot run from it, or hide from it, and you cannot ignore it. Dealing face to face with it is the only way to guarantee its defeat. Therefore, don't make up silly ineffective rules that ignore the real issue or problem. Just deal with it!

Because of the Jezebel spirit women are held responsible for the sexual climate of some churches. These churches have rules that stop women from wearing make-up, jewelry, pants, and they even have special dress codes. Theses rules are in enforced to keep women from "causing" the males of the church from being aroused, or distracted from their focus on the Lord. I seriously doubt on Judgment Day that the Lord is going to say to some man that He is not guilty of his sexual sins or immoral behavior because some woman made him do it. God did not say that to Adam. God did not hold Eve accountable for Adam's sin, He held Adam accountable and responsible for his own sin. God will hold every man, accountable for his own sins too.

In the Book of 1 Kings, God did not hold Jezebel accountable or responsible for the lack of leadership and stewardship on the part of King Ahab. King Ahab allowed idolatry and immorality to flourish in the Land-of-Israel, not Jezebel. King Ahab did not have the courage to stop Jezebel, but that's not Jezebel's fault. Jezebel was just being her demon possessed self. It was up to King Ahab to bring correction and punishment (idolatry was punishable by death under the Law of Moses) for Jezebel' behavior.

In the church today, the pastor is responsible and accountable for the spiritual condition of the congregation. Where the spirit of Jezebel is not addressed you can expect to find, immorality, pornography, homosexuality, other sexual perversities, teen pregnancy, teen rebellion, abortion, family separation, spouse abuse, child abuse, divorce, women refusing to be wives and mothers, or to raise their own children because their "call" in ministry is more important. Additionally, you will find a failure to establish and/or maintain a men's ministry (or a men's anything for that matter), and a constant loss of men who are called into ministry and leadership positions in the church. If that is not enough, women will be the head of practically every major ministry.

In churches where the Jezebel spirit is unchecked, there will be and atmosphere of fear and animosity toward men. The pastor may even surround himself with "males" who admire him, but they are afraid to speak up to him. These males will sing his praises no matter how debasing the situations become. They will look the other way in order not to offend the Jezebel, (if these men are on church staff it could cost them their jobs). Also, these males will avoid confronting even sin issues or put the pastor in a position in which he has to deal with the problem. How sad and unfulfilling it must be to "serve" under those conditions.

The Jezebel spirit is a problem because leadership will refuse to address it. The Jezebel spirit is a full blown attack by Satan against women. This Satanic attack could not possibly succeed in church or marriage without the full cooperation of the pastor or leader or head of household. It is an attack against the church as well as marriage and family, and God's established commands for marriage and family. *"Wives, submit to your own husbands as to the Lord"* (Ephesians 5:22) is not a suggestion, it is a command. Rebellion is a sin rooted in disobedience to the Word of God. Its purpose is to steal, kill, and destroy God ordained churches, marriages, and relationships. Rebellion disguised as a Jezebel spirit has one focus and that is to destroy women as wives, mothers, and ministers in the Body of Christ.

God commands all believers not to tolerate sin in any form. The rebellious attacks against the church are no different. It is completely up to the leadership of the church to carry out God's commands for the church. There are no acceptable excuses for not carrying out God's commands. Uncorrected or un-addressed rebellion and disobedience always leads to sin. Uncorrected or un-addressed sins will always proliferate. If any of the above mentioned sins in the paragraphs above are in your church, then be prepared to deal with the root cause. It will not go away on its own. The pastor, leaders, or husbands must deal with it, face to face.

Ephesians 5:27 says, *"that He might present her (the Body of Christ) to Himself a glorious church, not having spot or wrinkle or any such thing, but that she should be holy and without blemish."* A church with an unabated Jezebel spirit is anything but a church without spot, wrinkle, or blemish. Please take this passage seriously. You don't have to start a witch hunt. The Jezebel spirit is obvious, it is bold and outspoken. Deal with it in private or deal with it in public, but deal with it in accordance with the Word of God in Matthew 18:15-18.

The Book of Revelation 2:18-23 sums it all up, as God brings correction to the church of Thyatira. In verse 20 it says, *"that woman Jezebel, who calls herself a prophetess, to teach and seduce My servants to commit sexual immorality and eat things sacrificed to idols..."* and verse 22, *"indeed I will cast her into a sickbed, and those who commit adultery with her into great tribulations, unless they repent of their deeds."* In verse 21 the Lord says He gave her time to repent. God is giving churches time to act. Act before it is too late and God's judgment arrives.

As I have stated repeatedly, Satan hates humanity. He will steal, kill, and destroy at every opportunity that he is given. Satan is only one creature, but the demons are in the millions. Take this opportunity to become more aware of the enemy that you are fighting. Once you know you're under attack act and pray. God only fights the battles on the battlefields that you step onto. If you are in doubt or fear, then you have not and you will not step onto your battlefield. Remember, the enemy will not go away unless you send him away in the name of Jesus. You give the order and God will enforce it. *"The effective, fervent prayer of a righteous man (or church) avails much"* James 5:16.

Setting God's Priorities in Life

As I close this chapter, I cannot leave out one of the most successful tactics that the enemy uses to attack the family. This tactic can go unnoticed until the problem becomes so serious that family separation and even divorce may follow. It is involvement in church ministry. It is good to hear pastors warning their members not to get involved in more than one ministry and if that ministry gets in the way of your family, then step back and resolve the family problems. However, there are churches that actually teach their members that ministry comes before their families because they are working for God. Ministry never comes before anyone's family life. Even those in the fivefold ministry must realize that their family comes first. Your marriage is a vowed relationship between you, your spouse, and God. Your calling is between you and God, and it is not vowed by you, but assigned to you by God. Your first ministry is to your family, period.

I have seen so many people working sixty, eighty, or even a hundred hours each week as church staff members. They are told that they are sowing these hours to the Lord. They are even told that this overtime is their ministry. Also, what is even worse is that they are often paid minimum wage or a little above. They are also the first members that the church pressures for a pledge for some project. Of course, they are expected to find someone to take care of their children or spouse because God needs them at church. What is actually happening is they are being ripped off by their church. Yes, that is what I said. The shepherd who is supposed to be looking out for them is ripping them off in their family time and in their wages. Some of them are even on welfare (unless there is a church rule about them not getting on welfare because it would embarrass the church).

I am not talking about churches that are starting out and everybody wants to sacrifice some time and effort to assist in getting the church ministry off the ground. In this case, the pastor is working even more hours and is probably not getting paid or receiving very little. No, I am talking about well-established churches that have far too many people on staff to begin with and most of them are underpaid. Do not be surprised to find that most of these workers are untrained in the job that they are doing and are expected to learn as they go, never receiving any formal training. For many, they started out as volunteers, just lending a hand in support of the church. Of course, good volunteers are hard to find, so pay them something in order to keep them around. Soon after they are being paid, they can be used almost anywhere they are needed.

Let me clarify something: Being on a church staff does not mean that you have been called into ministry; being <u>hired</u> on staff means that you are an employee of the church. There are labor laws that must be followed. Withholding overtime pay and calling it a sacrifice is a sin. You are deceiving your employees. I know that one of the benefits is that they can get head-of-the-line privileges for marriage counseling, but the marriage counseling should never have been needed. They do not need marriage counseling, they need to be involved in <u>their marriages</u> and with <u>their families</u> more than they are involved in <u>the church</u>. It is a sin to treat church members this way and it is only a matter of time before the consequences of this sin catches up to the church. *5 "And I will come near you for judgment; I will be a swift witness against sorcerers, against adulterers, against perjurers, <u>against those who exploit wage earners</u> and widows and* *orphans, and against those who turn away an alien because they do not fear Me."* (Malachi 3:5)

Church employees should be paid more than their counterparts in the secular world. Some pastors make comparable salaries to executives in the secular world with organizations of similar size, and they should. Likewise, the employees should be treated the same. There is nothing wrong if they work extra on a project from time to time, and I am sure that they would gladly volunteer to do that. I am talking about employees who work extra hours every day and even weekends, and are now expected to do it as a rule. Hire people on staff as you would hire anyone for a job.

They should first and foremost be qualified for the job (what a concept) and then paid an above-average wage or salary because they work for the Body of Christ. Pastors do not hesitate to give large honorariums, $5,000 to $15,000.00 or more, to speakers for a few hours of ministry. Praise God that they do and can afford to do that. By the same token, ensure that the employees of the church are also well compensated for the daily work that they do for their church.

"For God will bring every work into judgment,
Including every secret thing, Whether good or evil."
Ecclesiastes 12:14

I hope that this word is a blessing to churches as well as to their employees. The same mentality that kept pastors poor and struggling over the years is keeping church employees "suffering for the Lord" on church staffs. In these End Times, there will be a great falling away of the church and it will not only be because of the sin of the members, but also because of injustice within the church itself.

The family is the building block of the church. Christian churches that stress family values, parenting, and child rearing will grow and prosper rapidly. Even non-Christian churches that build on these values are growing. Husbands, love your wives; parents, love your children and raise them up in the proper way; and, children honor and obey your parents are laws of God and they will work for whoever applies them. Shouldn't it be the Body of Christ that applies these laws?

Family growth, as well as church growth, does not happen by accident, it takes adherence to the Word of God and common sense application for His Word. There are no secrets to having a successful family life, because all of the answers have been written down in the Bible, and all you have to do is read them and apply them to your life.

God loves families. It is God who established families and He set them into churches. They belong to Him. Churches must take the time to teach their members how to be Christian families. Strong families build strong churches. The family unit will eventually determine if a church stands or falls. On the road to self-worth, strong family values are mandatory.

Praise the Lord!

***

CHAPTER SIX
RELATIONSHIPS

"I do not pray for these alone, but also for those who will believe in Me through their word; that they all may be one as You, Father, are in Me, and I in You; that they also may be one in Us that the world may believe that You sent Me. And the glory which You gave Me I have Given them, that they may be one just as We are one."
(John 17:20-21)

How can anyone be in a successful relationship and not understand who they are? If you were asked who you are, what would you say? I am sure many people believe they know who they are. Yet, if you ask various people who already know you, who they think you are, they would all give a different answer. So, if different people see you differently, then who truly knows who you are? Does anyone truly know who you are? The answer to this question is, definitely, yes. Other people know exactly who you are. You are defined by their beliefs, not yours. Your beliefs about yourself are too often swayed by the image you're using that day. Other people see through your images and accept you for who they believe you to be, in spite of your images. People know you by what you say, but they define you by what you do.

It is a common belief that other people have to "get to know you first" before they can truly say who you are as a person. Listen, you do not exist outside of who other people define you to be. In other words, without other people, you don't exist! You do not live in a void. If people have to "get to know you first," then who did they meet? What you do they need to know? So, who do other people say you are? If it resembles God's definition of you, then you are on the right path.

Somewhere, there has to be a foundation or source for who you are that you can depend on to be 100 percent true. That foundation and source is the Bible, the Word of God. The Bible clearly defines who you are in both the Old and the New Testaments. You may already know this to be true, but it does not mean you accept it. You may need to hear it over and over again before you'll receive it in

125

your heart and make it a part of your belief system. God is the "other person" who defines who you are, in spite of your images.

Did you ever wonder why God created mankind in the first place? When you read His Word in the Bible, you will find out that God has a burning desire to be in relationship with His most loved creation, mankind. God had already created the angels, and they were of all sizes, shapes, and power. However, they could not fulfill God's desire to fellowship with His creations.

In Genesis chapter 1, God says, *"Let <u>Us</u> make man in <u>Our</u> image and according to <u>Our</u> likeness"* (Genesis 1:26). God created mankind in His image and likeness so that He could relate to them as a Father to His children, and not just as a Creator to His creation. God desires to be Father and <u>Daddy</u> to His children. *"For you did not receive the spirit of bondage again to fear, but you received the Spirit of <u>adoption</u> by whom we cry out, <u>Abba, Father</u>. [16]The Spirit Himself bears witness with our spirit that we are <u>children of God</u>, [17]and if <u>children</u>, then <u>heirs</u>—heirs of God and <u>joint heirs with Christ</u>, if indeed we suffer with Him, that we may also be glorified together"* (Romans 8:15-17). God sees His children just as He sees Jesus. He expects us to be one just as He is one with Jesus. All of His children are heirs or partakers of all of God's goodness.

Let me be perfectly clear about the Father's children. They are the "seed" of Abraham who by faith believe in Jesus as the Son of God, who died for our sins, rose from the dead and is our Savior and Redeemer. God's children are called Christians because they follow the Word of God which is Jesus Christ. His Word is written in the Bible, translated from Aramaic, Hebrew, and Greek. His Word is not a religious doctrine or a theological treatise or a dogmatic theory derived from some privileged intellectual discourse. But His Word is truth. It is alive and powerful and filled with revelation knowledge.

> *For the word of God is living and powerful,*
> *and sharper than any two-edged sword, piercing*
> *even to the division of soul and spirit, and of joints*
> *and marrow, and is a discerner of the thoughts and*
> *intents of the heart." Hebrews 4:12*

God does everything decently and in order, including establishing His family or Body of Believers here on Earth. *"Let all things be done decently and in order" (I Corinthians 14:40)*. He did not decide one day to make mankind His children. He created mankind to be His children from the beginning. However, mankind still has their free will option of choosing Him as Father. God, the Father allows you to use your free will to choose or reject Him. God laid out clear-cut paths and directions for choosing membership in His family. To ensure that everyone would not be confused about the process, He used inspired writers to record His desires.

There are more people who have heard the Word of God, than those who have read His Word in the Bible. If you have heard it preached, then you must take the opportunity to read it for yourself. If someone preaches a false interpretation of His Word and you believe it because you would not read it for yourself, then you are responsible for your false belief(s). On Judgment Day, you will be standing there all by yourself with no one to blame or point to. You will be held accountable for your beliefs as well as your unbelief.

All Scripture is given by inspiration of God, and is
profitable for doctrine, for reproof, for correction,
for instruction in righteousness, ¹⁷that the man
of God may be complete, thoroughly equipped
for every good work." II Timothy 3:16-17

I said all of that to say, your relationship with God is up to you as an individual. God has NO grandchildren! Every relationship with God is individual. You may belong to a church body, but each member is still an individual to God. Read the Bible for yourself. No one has a perfect understanding of the Bible because God does not require anyone to have one. God is not seeking perfection, but He is seeking a personal relationship with each one of you. Just like your relationship with parents or siblings, you may all be in the same family, but your relationships with your parents and siblings are all different from person to person. That is exactly the way it is with God. Just follow God's example in the relationship He had with His Son, Jesus. Jesus called Him **Father**, not mother or uncle or anything else. Jesus called Him **Father**. Follow the example Jesus gave and you will gain clarity in your relationship with the Father.

God does everything for a specific purpose. When God wants something, He sows a seed in order to receive it. He wanted a universe, so He spoke the words or seeds of faith, and a universe was created. Hebrews 11:1 says, *"Now faith is the substance of things hoped for and the evidence of things not seen."* That substance of faith is the spoken word. Jesus is the substance of faith. He is the Word of God. The things that God spoke of, by faith, materialized. His words of faith became tangible evidence, or proof, of their existence in the spirit realm of faith. That same faith that God spoke by is available to each and every one of His children. God's order is clear and it does not waver. It does not change because of new beliefs or public opinion. Therefore, if you find out what God has to say about being in relationship with Him, you can take it to the bank. You can stand on it for life. No one can deceive you about it or change your mind about it unless you allow them to. God's Word is His bond, forever.

The first thing that must be done is easiest. God created mankind, so He knew He had to keep it simple. In order to be His child, you must simply accept Jesus as your Lord and Savior. Again, you must believe in your heart that Jesus is the Son of God and He died for your sins, rose from the dead, and is now in heaven with the Father and confess it with you mouth (say it). Until you can accept the Son of God, Jesus, you cannot be a part of the kingdom that God has for His children. *"Jesus said to him, I am the way, the truth, and the life. No one comes to the Father except through Me"* (John 14:6). If you cannot believe that Jesus is the Son of God, then how could you ever believe that you are a child of God?

In the world, many people believe that there is a God, but not everyone believes in His Son, Jesus. How can God the Father be real to you? How can God the Creator be real to you? How can anything that requires faith be real to anyone that believes only in what they see? It does require faith to believe in God, in the Creator, in His Son, Jesus. Faith is the link, the password that opens the door that leads into the family of God. Jesus is the door, and it is a narrow door because no one can fit through it covered in the armor of unbelief. It is faith that removes the armor of unbelief and exposes the heart to the enlightenment of the Word of God, who is Jesus Christ.

I started out by saying that this is the easy part because it only takes believing, not works or acts or some secret code. Choose to believe or not to believe, it is that simple. Again, it is all written for you to read for yourself. If you truly want a personal relationship with the Father, then simply do what He says to do, believe in His Son, Jesus.

The Tithe

God the Father is a jealous God. He will not tolerate any other god. He has given His Body of Believers various methods to test to see if they are truly His children. One of these tests is the **tithe**. If you truly believe in God as Father and Creator, then what is the problem about obeying His word concerning the tithe? If God is the Creator and He created everything, including money, then simply obey His word. God will never ask you for anything that He has not already given to you. Therefore, He never asks for anything that you do not have in your possession. You never have to go into debt in order to obey God in your giving. Use that as a rule for your giving. If you have to take out a loan or borrow the money or "**PLEDGE**" money you do not have, then **IT IS NOT A WORD FROM GOD.** I know that statement will cause uproar in some churches, but it is the truth. It is stated in Proverbs 22:26, *"Do not be one of those who shakes hands in a pledge, one of those who is surety for debts..."*

God does NOT need your money! This is a test and it is only a test of your obedience. Is God your Lord or is money your lord? Pick one! God expects His children to be possessors not borrowers. The tithe is 10 percent of everything you have earned through your gifts, talents, and skills. Who gave you your gifts, talents, and skills? You must earn seed, not steal it, borrow it, or beg for it. If all of the money that you have received in a certain timeframe has been given to you, then there is no tithe due on it. Welfare is an example of that. You do not earn welfare checks, it is given to you. (Please do not hear this as a putdown for people who receive welfare assistance. If you need it, then receive it. However, don't let it become a way of life for you.) If you do earn some amount of money during this season of receiving welfare, then do not hesitate to pay your tithe on that money and sow a seed from it also.

Malachi 3:8-12 is clear, to the point and does not compromise in any way the message of paying the tithing and giving an offering (sowing a seed).

8 *"Will a man <u>rob</u> God? Yet you have robbed Me! But you say, in what way have we robbed You? In <u>tithes</u> and <u>offerings</u>.*
9 *You are <u>cursed</u> with a curse, for you have robbed Me, even this whole nation.*
10 *Bring <u>all the tithes</u> into the <u>storehouse</u>, that there may be food in <u>My house</u>, and <u>try Me [TEST ME]</u> now in this, says the LORD of hosts, If I will not open for you the <u>windows of heaven</u> and pour out for you such blessing that <u>there will not be room enough to receive it</u>.*
11 *And I will <u>rebuke the devourer</u> for your sakes, So that he will not <u>destroy the fruit of your ground</u>, Nor shall the <u>vine fail to bear fruit</u> for you in the field, says the LORD of hosts;*
12 *And all nations will call you <u>blessed</u>, for you will be a <u>delightful land</u>, says the LORD of hosts."*

God's word was not just for the Old Testament. The prophecy given to the Prophet Malachi was the last word that the Lord would speak to His people for over 400 years. He was giving them one more opportunity to get in right standing with Him. Of all the things that the Lord spoke on, it was the tithe that received most of His attention. The Father did not want money to be a lord over His people or over His children. Is money your lord? Do you obey your wallet or purse or do you obey the Lord? It really is that simple.

Satan would never do anything to get you to support the Body of Christ. He certainly would not want you to provide financial support that would lead to church growth. So, who do you think is telling you not to tithe or sow seeds? Tithing is a God thing yesterday, today, and for as long as you are on the Earth. Do not let your money come between you and God. Do not be a robber! Would you bless someone who robs you every payday? Would you be there for that person when they call out for your help? No you would not and neither would God.

The tithe is **10 percent,** not 9 percent or 11 percent, but **10 percent**. I don't know why believers have such a hard time with this. I do know that disciples do not. You do not even need a calculator to figure out 10 percent. Just do it out of your obedience. When you leave for Sunday morning service, you already know what the tithe amount is for your earnings. You may not know how much of an offering you will give to the church. God will tell you through the Holy Spirit. It will probably be the amount that you hear in your heart, but do not want to give. However, it will be an amount that you do possess. Remember, God will not ask you for anything that you do not possess. If you are obedient in your giving (only you and God will ever know), then you should expect a blessing from God in return. This blessing will be in the form of money AND many other things. It is all right to expect a blessing from the Lord; He tells you to expect it. God, the Lord, even tells you to "test" Him to see if this is true in Malachi 8:10.

The tithe is the first test of your true relationship with the Lord. The tithe is a test of your obedience and acceptance of God as Father. The tithe is a type of the "Tree of the Knowledge of Good and Evil" that tempted Adam and Eve in the Garden of Eden. God said do not touch it or eat it, but the enemy tempts you with it every opportunity he can get. Do not touch or eat the tithe. It does not belong to you. Do not let money be your lord, and do not obey its commands to rob God. Pursue a personal relationship with the Father not on your term, but on His terms.

The tithe is paid to God through the church in which you are a member. The tithe is between you and God. It is the pastor's responsible to teach you how to tithe, but it is not the pastor's personal business whether you tithe or not. It is WRONG to have people bring in their W-2 forms to verify their tithing records, or bring a pay stub to prove to their pastor they are tithing. What is the real purpose of checking up on church members? Malachi 3:8 says, will a man rob

God, not will a man rob the pastor or rob the church. It is no one's business who is tithing or not. It is certainly no one's business how much anyone gives to the church.

I had to bring up those points because money has become the evaluator or who is eligible to receive from the church. If a church member does not have a proven track record of tithing and giving to the church, then they are ineligible to receive from the church in their time of need. This same church would give food and money to people and organizations that they don't know before they would even help a church member who is not considered faithful in their giving. Don't sit in judgment of them, be careful. They are God's people not the pastor's. God sent them to support the ministry He called the pastor into. God sent them to be fed by you not fleeced. Be careful!

This issue of receiving tithes and offerings has caused problems in many churches. Some pastors will not teach on the tithe or offerings because they are afraid of offending the congregation. It is God's Word and a command, therefore it must be taught. Teach on the tithe and offerings so that the congregation can be blessed. (I visited a church where the pastor ordered the church Elders to stand by the doors during offering. If the offering is not the amount that he wanted he continued to ask for more money until he reached his goal. The Elders are by the door to make sure no one leaves until all the money is collected.) If that should ever happen to you, call the police because you have just been robbed.

I have heard worse stories. Since I only heard about them I won't write about them. Just teach the truth and have faith and God will meet all of the needs of the church. Money is a lord, don't let it become yours.

Sowing Seed (offering)

What a glorious and wonderful God you serve. He blesses you with even more than you bless Him because of your obedience. Luke 6:38 says, *"Give and it will be given to you: good measure, pressed down, shaken together, and running over __will be__ put into your bosom. For with the same measure that you use, it will be measured back to you."* Also in Genesis 26:12-13 it says, *[12]"Then Isaac sowed in that land, and reaped in the same year a hundredfold; and the LORD blessed him. [13]The man began to prosper, and continued prospering until he became very prosperous."*

Do not let anyone tell you not to have an expectation from the Lord for your giving. If you tell your children to do something for you and to expect a reward when they are done, do you think that they are expecting you to keep your word? Of course they are, and they are excited about receiving their reward. No father will love you more and reward you more than your Father in heaven.

When you attend a church service, you go to receive from the Lord. It is a time of receiving from the Word of God. No one expects to go the church to receive and to return home in debt. That's why I said that a pledge to give is not a word from God. I did not say it is evil or even wrong to do it, but is it God's way of bringing in financial support? God does not need to put you in debt in order to get you to give. As a Christian, you should fast, pray and ask God for what you need. God brings the increase, so that you can do the things that cost money to do.

If the church needs to raise money for a project, then the church should come together as a whole as fast, pray, and ask God for the money. God MUST answer your prayers. He will certainly provide the increase for the Body of Christ in order that their tithe and giving will increase and provide every dime that is needed. Pray in the increase, not pressure in the increase.

God does not burden his children with debt, and the local church should not do it either. I have to bring out this point because too many churches practice taking up pledges. People who can afford to pledge will either give a lump sum that they already have (not go into debt) or they will give a weekly or monthly amount that they know they can afford from their paychecks. However, those who "want" to pledge, but know they do not have the money will pledge anyway in hope that God will bring the increase to pay this debt. When the money does not show up, then God is to blame, or maybe there is something they are doing wrong or unresolved sin in their lives, etc.

The pledge ends up bringing condemnation on too many people. This is not God's best or His way.

Additionally, pledges cause far too many people to leave the church because of how they feel about not fulfilling their pledge. They "owe" the church and they did not pay. If they did not borrow money from the church, then how could they possibly owe the church anything? The pledge is not biblical. It is man's way of raising money, but it is not God's way. Instead of asking or begging the members for more and more money, why don't you teach them how to have faith for the money? Speak the money into existence as God has taught the Body to do, not beg it into existence. (I know that I have just disqualified myself from ministering in thousands of churches.)

If your church is on a pledge campaign, then come before God and ask Him for the money as I have described, as a Body of believers, as His children. Watch and see what the Lord will do. Watch the increase flow in among the congregation and then observe their faithfulness when they bring the increase into the storehouse. They will be blessed exceedingly abundantly above all they could ask or think, and so will the church. I say all of this to be a blessing to all of God's church congregations, not to bring condemnation. Just give God's way a try for a few months and see if more money comes flooding in than ever before. Also, be in expectation of someone coming to your church, a person sent by God who may just hand you a check for the entire amount you are taking up pledges for. God is His Word and His Word is named Jesus. Just trust Him!

The Holy Spirit's Prayer Language – Tongues

God wants relationships with His children. He wants right relationships with His children. No matter what the situation is right now, God can turn it around and make it better. If things are not going according to your plan, then check and see if you are acting in accordance with God's plan for your life. God is in constant pursuit of each one of His children. The farther you pull away from the Lord, the harder the pursuit God has for you. Draw nearer and nearer to the

Lord every day through prayer, fasting and spending personal time with Him. Pray often throughout the day and if you do not have your prayer language (praying in tongues) then just ask Him and He will certainly give it to you. You will never grow as close to the Lord in your own understanding as you can or will in His understanding.

The Lord gave the Body of Christ His prayer language through the Holy Spirit (I Corinthians 14) and far too many do not accept it. It is in the New Testament. The New Testament is the only testament or covenant that Christians have, so what part of it is not for Christians? What part of it is not for today? Today is still covered by the New Testament, so take it all. There is power in your prayer language, immeasurably more than in your own understanding. God wants a personal relationship with His children.

Trust the Father with all of your heart and do not depend on your own understanding. Free fall with the Lord and He will surely deliver you from all of your troubles. For His Word says,

> 8 *"For My thoughts are not your thoughts,*
> *Nor are your ways My ways," says the LORD.*
> 9 *"For as the heavens are higher than the Earth,*
> *So are My ways higher than your ways,*
> *And My thoughts than your thoughts."*
> 10 *"For as the rain comes down, and the snow from heaven,*
> *And do not return there,*
> *But water the Earth,*
> *And make it bring forth and bud,*
> *That it may give seed to the sower*
> *And bread to the eater,*
> 11 *"So shall My word be that goes forth from My mouth;*
> *It shall not return to Me void,*
> *But it shall accomplish what I please,*
> *And it shall prosper in the thing for which I sent it."*
> *Isaiah 55:8-11*

Stand on the Word of God. Obey His commands and He will uphold all that He has promised. Have a right relationship with the

Lord. Of course, this includes the money that He gives to you through your gifts, talents, skills. This is the money you earn. No one should have to look over your shoulder to see if you are being obedient in your giving. Don't cheat God. If you do, God will know, you will know, and the devil will know. Don't let the devil use your disobedience to God's command against you. Be instantly faithful with all your money so that the devil cannot get a foothold into your life.

4-Stages of Relationships (Another Point of View)

Honeymoon – Conflict – Communication – Growth
Stages of Relationships

I hope that I did not lose too many people in the last few pages. I suppose if you have gotten this far, then you will stick with me to the end. I know that some of the things that I have written about are not well received, especially when you first read it. Maybe, after a few days of meditating on it, you may change your mind and give it a second chance. Remember, God will not change for anyone. He is the same God all the time. I provided scriptures so that you can see for yourself and decide if you agree with my interpretation. If not, that is okay. This is about your personal relationship with the Lord. It is surely different from my relationship, and that is just the way the Lord planned it. As long as we can agree that Jesus is Lord, then we can live with the rest.

As you continue to read this book, you will notice that we are developing our own personal relationship. It will be strictly based on your beliefs. However, it will still be subject to the four stages of all relationships.

As I was saying, we have already entered into a relationship. It started in the first stage (honeymoon), just as all relationships do, and rapidly evolved into the other three stages as you read each chapter. It happens in all relationships. Some take longer than others to go through all four stages and many do not make it past the second stage (conflict). I know there are many books and articles on the stages of relationships. I like the four that I present here (and in the Marriage chapter) because they are easy to remember and most importantly they make sense. They are all a part of "getting to know" another person. Human beings are complex creatures, and that is the way God wanted it. Your complexity keeps you unique and therefore, each person has a personal relationship with the Lord.

When you bought this book, our relationship was in the honeymoon stage. It could have been in the conflict stage because someone told you not to buy it for various reasons. Maybe they did not like it or had problems with some of the things that I wrote. They influenced your opinion before you even read one word of it. However, before they influenced you, you may not have had an opinion one way or another. The honeymoon stage is like that; it is the beginning of all relationships "before" you gather enough negative information (from any source) about that person.

The conflict stage happens when you find something that you do not like or agree with in a person. As you read this book, you may have found things you did not like and still do not agree with, so the conflict began. If you read on and found a reason to resolve the issue, then communication was able to be restored and the conflict was no longer great enough to stop you from continuing. As you read on, you began to pick out certain areas that you could agree with, but you still may not agree on others, then the growth stage began as you moved on with an understanding beyond who is right or wrong.

As I said before, I believe that all relationships go through these stages, including our relationship with God. Some certainly do not move beyond the conflict stage, because you decide that the conflict is irreconcilable, so the relationship ends right there. That is the way people are with God.

Stage one: People get saved and are filled with joy and love and even forgiveness. Their burdens are gone and their hearts free. They can even laugh, cry, and share their testimony. The future appears bright and everything seems to be alright. They thank God for loving them and not giving up on them.

Stage two: The new believers discover that they can no longer live in sin and be in a right relationship with God, so conflict raises its ugly head. They may look for ways to make God's Word fit their situation, at least for a season, because they don't want to go all the way back to their old way of behaving. When they cannot manipulate the Word, they turn from it and begin to look in all the wrong places for the answers that God had already set right in front of them. (Like the activist for the homosexual lifestyle [death style], decided to do to make the Bible fit his beliefs; he cut out every scripture that he found to be against the practice of homosexuality. Now, he believed he could have a real relationship with the Lord—on his terms. In reality, he has created division between himself and God. If you bring God down to your level, then you are god and He is now your servant. This is called "religion.")

Stage three: New believers learn to pray and attend church regularly to hear the Word of God. They find ways to work out their differences with God. They even begin to give up some of the desires of the flesh and notice changes in their lives. They are even thankful for the changes in their lives and begin to openly share their testimony with others.

Stage four: New believers begin to grow in their relationship with God because of the Word. Their pursuit is not only for themselves, but for others. They begin to see themselves as disciples and look for opportunities to share the Gospel with others. The call that is on their lives becomes apparent to those around them. The Holy Spirit is now able to have a direct impact on their lives and blesses them with His anointed gifts, I Corinthians 12.

Of course, conflict returns often to challenge their new beliefs and the need to battle through into the communication stage once again arises. As long as they are willing to battle through the conflicts, no matter what it takes, they will continue to communicate with the Lord and grow in His Word. However, when a conflict presents itself as "I am right and God's Word is wrong" or simply as a choice not to obey God's Word, then the relationship ends right there in the conflict stage.

If you are in unresolved conflict with the Lord, then you have backslidden, gone back to your old beliefs. Backsliders are stuck in the conflict stage with God's Word. It is not a conflict with a person, although they may direct their anger toward a person or blame a person for their backslidden condition. The truth is they are in conflict with God and that is a choice. When they decide to come back to the Lord, no one can stop them, not even the person they blamed. All relationships with God are personal, one on one. God will always maintain His part and stand on His Word; His Word will not change for anyone. Once they have learned this vital lesson, they can stand on His Word and it will not let them down.

Honeymoon Stage of Relationships

The honeymoon stage does not mean love at first sight. It is the honeymoon stage because you do not have enough information to base a negative opinion against someone yet. The person is new to you, so it is safe to accept them as they are. This situation can change rapidly. After a few encounters, you begin to see yourself in them and with that revelation, you begin to see all the things you do not like about yourself in them. They become a mirror that reminds you of your faults, scars, bruises, hurts, and worst of all, your secrets. Of course, they're the same and you are the one who has begun to change. You cannot see it because you are not open to feedback from anyone. That wonderful honeymoon stage is ending and it is not your fault.

The honeymoon stage can last too long. You can refuse to accept the reality of your relationship with someone you "love," even when the evidence is presented. What evidence could possibly turn your heart away from the person you have professed your love to? For some people, even when abuse begins—physical, mental, or emotional—they will not leave their dream world and face reality. Even though the honeymoon stage ended and the conflict is at its worst; and they will not accept it.

The honeymoon stage is simply the first stage of any relationship. You need to know that it will not last as it is. God made people to be attracted to each other. He expects them to communicate with each other and to grow in their relationship. No one can hold onto the past and grow in the things of God. Your relationships should be dynamic and alive, not stale, tired, and predictable. Know that you know the relationship is supposed to change and grow and look different from when it started. Fully expect changes and welcome them first in yourself and secondly in others.

Conflict Stage of Relationships

To everything there is a season,
A time for every
purpose under heaven:
⁵ A time to embrace,
And a time to refrain
from embracing...
⁷ A time to keep silence,
And a time to speak...
⁸ A time to love,
And a time to hate;
A time of war
And a time of peace."
Ecclesiastes 3:1, 5, 7-8

Everything must change if it is to live and grow. The flesh hates change. The five senses bring in information for the mind and body. The mind and body will fight against doing anything differently from what it has already experienced. That is why a habit is so hard to break when it is connected to the flesh. The mind and body will continue to do things and desire things, even if they are harmful or deadly to the flesh. It is only by the spirit that you are that change is possible. The carnal mind of your flesh will always be at war with the spirit.

As Christians, you must be keenly aware of the war between the flesh and the spirit. Romans 8:5-8 says, ⁵*"For those who live according to the flesh set their minds on the things of the flesh,*

but those who live according to the Spirit, the things of the Spirit.
⁶For to be carnally minded is death, but to be spiritually minded is
life and peace. ⁷ Because the carnal mind is enmity against God;
for it is not subject to the law of God, nor indeed can be. ⁸ So then,
those who are in the flesh cannot please God."

The conflict stage is a battle against the flesh. Every human
being has a need to be right. Just how a person goes about being
right differs from one person to another, based on their personality.
Because the conflict is resistance to change, it cannot be avoided.
Change will happen with or without your cooperation. In actuality,
God is revealing something in your heart that He wants to heal. He
only reveals to heal you, not to hurt you.

During conflict character is developed. Does anger, wrath,
violence, lying, tantrums, or other expressions of rebellion and
discontent emerge during the conflict? Just how much control or
authority do you have over yourself? If it is very little, then it is
because your focus is on someone else and not yourself. Once the
focus is turned inward, then the solution will become apparent. The
conflict is in you, not in someone else. Character is developed by
how you handle the conflict. It is brought out in the solution, not in
the conflict itself.

Since no two people are alike, there will always be conflicts.
Expect conflicts and be ready to handle them, not run from them.
As you build character, you will be better equipped to deal with each
and every problem that comes along. Of course it is only through the
Word of God that you are able to develop the character. The character
that you are building is the character of Jesus. Let the Word of God
do the work for you. Use the Word, prayer, and fasting to work
through conflicts each time they arise. Do not depend on your own
understanding or on secular methods and techniques. Keep in mind
that the conflict stage is only a season of change; just how long the
season lasts is entirely up to you.

The conflict stage should be shortest of the four stages.
Unfortunately, conflict is too often the longest. Long-term friendships
are abandoned, sibling rivalries take root, parents and children destroy
their relationships, and divorce takes place in the conflict stage. The

need to be right outweighs the wedding vows and overshadows the love you said that you had for each other. Remember, you must first have a break in your relationship with God before you can have a break in your relationship with your spouse.

Take a stand on the Word of God and do not let any conflict cause you to give up. Fight and push forward by taking responsibility for your actions and words. Be quick to forgive, even if you do not feeeeeel like it. Even if you are not at fault, be ready to apologize or forgive. Value the relationship more than your self-righteousness. If you do forgive and truly value the relationship, then moving beyond the conflict will become the rule and not the exception. You will also notice that you have just entered the communication stage of your relationship.

Communication Stage of Relationships

[11] "For whoever exalts himself will be humbled,
and he who humbles himself will be exalted."
Luke 14:11

Have you ever experienced humility? You cannot fake humility; you cannot "**do**" humility. You must "**be**" humble. Humility is excellence, where being right is perfection. Excellence builds and perfection destroys. Your willingness to surrender your point of view, even when you are right, takes humility. Without humility, you will never love anyone unconditionally. The flesh will rebel with all of its might against admitting you are wrong. It is not an easy thing to do. But if you keep in mind that it is a war between the spirit and the flesh, then you can take authority over the flesh and say the words that need to be said.

It's such a wonderful experience to be set free from self-righteousness. You experienced it when you received Jesus as your Lord and Savior. The conflict between you being right and the Word of God being right was finally resolved, at least for a season. This conflict is called self-righteousness. However, did you notice that conflicts increased as you pursued the Word of God? It took time with the Lord in prayer, fasting, and reading the Word before you were willing to surrender again. I hope that you understand that this is the way it will be as long as you are a human being. In the Gospel of John 16:33, Jesus said, *"These things I have spoken to you, that in Me you may have peace. In the world you will have tribulation; but be of good cheer, I have overcome the world."* Don't be intimidated by conflict, be prepared to overcome it in the name of Jesus.

The closer you become in your relationship with the Lord Jesus and the Holy Spirit, the easier it will be to enter the communication stage. You will become quick to hear the Lord's voice and quick to listen to His instructions. Just as the Word says in John 8:36, *"Therefore, if the Son makes you free, you shall be free indeed."* On the other hand, without the Son, freedom is not possible.

The communication stage is a time of discovery for your life. It is a time of transformation and renewing of the mind. As you take authority over your flesh and put down the rebellion of your mind, you will see yourself maturing in the things of God. Now, do not be deceived into thinking that you can grow close to God and not grow close to people. That is impossible! The whole purpose of Christian growth is to become a disciple of Jesus Christ. If you do not want to spend time with people, then who will you disciple?

The communication stage is the season to press in and reach for the things that God has planned for your life in the future. God's plan for your life will always include other people. The Apostle Paul says it best in his letter to the Philippians 3:13-14, **¹³"Brethren, I do not count myself to have apprehended; but one thing *I do,* forgetting those things which are behind and reaching forward to those things which are ahead, ¹⁴I press toward the goal for the prize of the upward call of God in Christ Jesus."** The upward call is simply to be quick and willing to tell someone about Jesus. The upward call is discipleship.

Be ready and willing to enter into the communication stage every time conflict arises. Do not spend time in strife, anger leading to wrath, or offense. Speak life by speaking forgiveness and when necessary, repentance. The more time you spend in this season of communication, the more growth you will see in all of your relationships.

Growth Stage of Relationships

[4]*"And they were all filled with the Holy Spirit
and began to speak with other tongues,
as the Spirit gave them utterance."*
Acts 2:4

Growth follows nourishment. Nourishment must be specific for a given situation. Baby food is mandatory for the early growth of a baby, but baby food cannot sustain a young child or a teenager. The same is true for relationships. Relationships must be properly fed. Relationships will not grow without the Word of God. The "love" that was there from the start will begin to dissipate as time passes on without the Word of God.

The initial attraction was not designed to hold a relationship together. It's the stuff dreams are made of. Unfortunately, you cannot live in a dream. You should welcome the change and growth, but not everyone does. For the young teen, that initial attraction is puppy love. For the young adult, it is often just plain old lust, a desire of the flesh. God made mankind to be attracted to each other (the opposite sex only). However, when that attraction is controlled by the flesh, it will lead to sin (adultery, fornication, and attraction to the same sex). But when that attraction is controlled by the spirit, it can grow and will produce unconditional love.

The growth stage of any relationship is built on the level of communication that you are willing to reach and the amount of change you are willing to make. If you are closed to change, then expect the relationship to eventually die out. If the change is slow and burdensome, then expect lots of conflict. However, if the relationship is open to change and pursues change from the Word of God, then expect great things to happen. There is no limit to the growth of a relationship that is hungry for the Word of God. Blessings will abound, and then love, joy, and peace will be the norm for your relationship. Keep the Word of God at the forefront of your relationship.

Consider the Apostles in the early days after the resurrection of Jesus. Jesus had risen into heaven and His Disciples were spending most of their time in hiding. It had only been a couple months earlier when they were casting out demons, healing the sick, and celebrating their "growth" in the Word. Jesus had fed them with manna, but the meat had yet to come. Their growth and power was dependent on their acceptance of the Holy Spirit whom Jesus said He would send to them after He had arisen into heaven. There were over 500 disciples after the resurrection, but by the Day of Pentecost, there were only 120. Their future growth still depended on what they did next. Jesus told them what to expect in order to continue as His Church, but it was up to them to do it.

> *[4]"And being assembled together with them,*
> *He commanded them not to depart from Jerusalem,*
> *but to wait for the Promise of the Father,*
> *'which,'" He said, 'you have heard from Me;*
> *[5]for John truly Baptized with water,*
> *but you shall be baptized with the <u>Holy Spirit</u>*
> *not many days from now.'*
> *[6]therefore, when they had come together,*
> *they asked Him, saying,*
> *'Lord, will You at this time restore the kingdom to Israel?' [7] And*
> *He said to them,*
> *It is not for you to know times or seasons*
> *which the Father has put in His own authority.*
> *[8]But you shall receive <u>POWER</u>*
> *when the <u>Holy Spirit</u> has come upon you;*
> *and you shall be witnesses to Me*
> *in Jerusalem, and in all Judea and Samaria,*
> *and to the end of the Earth."*
> *Acts 1:4-8*

In the growth stage, you will receive **power** to continue on and accomplish everything you need to do in your relationship with God. The growth stage for Christian relationships must include the Holy Spirit. How much time do you want to spend battling through conflicts? Yes, conflicts will come, but they do not have to last or destroy your relationship with God when they come. Arm yourself with **power** from the Holy Spirit in preparation for the battle. If you do, then you will be like the early church that added 3,000 souls on one occasion and 5,000 souls on another. Now that is growth. How much do you want your relationship with God to grow? It is up to you. Do not deny yourself anything that the Lord has provided for your life.

The growth stage is dynamic, it has no limit. The people who knew you before will not recognize you. And better still, you will not recognize yourself as the person you use to be. It is exciting to serve the Lord, but it is obligatory to continue to grow in His Word and guidance. Anytime you decide to stop pursuing His Word, then expect to see change for the worse. You cannot sustain growth in the natural or on your own ability. Like the saying goes, "Your talent can get you there, but it's your character that will keep you there." Your natural ability will never measure up to your God-given character. Let the Holy Spirit feed you and nourish you. Ask for your prayer language and receive it. Do not let anyone tell you that speaking in tongues is not from the Holy Spirit or not for today. Do not let tradition or false teaching keep you from completing your race. *44"While Peter was still speaking these words, the <u>Holy Spirit fell</u> upon all those who heard the word... 46For they heard them <u>speak with tongues</u> and magnify God."* (Acts 10:44, 46)

Today is all you have and it is more than enough when you are in the presence of the Lord. This life is not a practice session. There are no make-up exams. The results are final and the results are decided by you. Decide to stay out of the past and to live in the present. Learn to communicate, even when you do not feel like it. Be quick to forgive (forgiveness only happens in the present). Be a disciple of Jesus Christ and not a believer only.

The Reality of Relationships

I hope that by now you are getting a clearer picture of what relationships are all about. All relationships are based wholly on what you believe they are and what you <u>say</u> they are. I know other people are involved, but the only person who determines the quality of the relationships that they're in is you. You may want to believe that it is the other person who determines the quality of the relationship, as if you are just there for the ride, but it is never that way. The problem is that you do not recognize who you're being in your relationships. You act differently depending on who you are relating to. You act one way around Mom or Dad, another way around the boss, another way around your spouse, etc., etc., etc. How many of you are there and which one is really you? Therefore, if you do not know who you are, how can you know who is showing up, or participating in your relationships?

The reality of your relationships will always be based on who you decide to be. You must be in alignment with the Word of God; if not, you will be truly lost. God has written down exactly what He thinks about you and exactly how he made you to be. It is in the pursuit of God's Word that you discover exactly who you are. In that pursuit, you are forced to relate to people with integrity, honesty, humility, love, and truth, to name a few. It is in their "feedback" that you find out who you are. People are your mirror. If they are your mirror, then pick a mirror that is in pursuit of the same things you are, like the Lord Jesus Christ.

(<u>Feedback</u> is: An experience of someone stated in words, not a prior assessment, but a present experience. The difference between feedback and assessment is: An experience happens in the moment in the present; and an assessment is a fixed belief about someone based on the past. No matter what they do, you will not change your belief about that person. This person has become a final decision to you. It is now impossible for you to have an experience of them because they only exist in your past memory.)

Before you were saved, being around someone you knew was a Christian brought conviction because of your behavior. If you have a sin problem with vulgar language and a minister comes around, you become conscious of every word you say. If you have a sin problem with pornography and a minister comes around, you get busy hiding the evidence. These various people are mirrors. It is not them, but the reflection of yourself that you see in them. They help to validate who you are. Are you comfortable in the company of sinners? If you are, then they are the feedback that validates your lifestyle. Are you comfortable in the company of God-loving and God-fearing men and women? Again, they are your feedback.

Here is an exercise to help you see the points that I have been trying to make. <u>Please follow the directions to the letter</u>. (**You will need an approximately one hour to complete this exercise.**)

1. On a scale of 1 to 10, with <u>1</u> being the best and <u>10</u> being the worst, measure the following relationships as you see them TODAY. If one or more of the examples do not apply, then leave it blank. Fill in all of the blanks that apply to you. <u>DO</u> NOT fill in the final blank (located at the end of the chapter) until you are directed to do so. Do not read anything into this exercise. Answer each question with complete honesty and candor. Remember, God only reveals things in our lives in order to heal us.

2. Place a number from 1 to 10 on the line following the name of the person(s) with whom you have or had a relationship. There are extra lines for brothers and sisters, etc., in case you want to measure each person. However, you can give a general measure to all of your brothers or sisters on one line. Measure the relationships, base it on how you see the relationship <u>TODAY</u>, <u>right now</u> in the <u>present moment</u>. It does not matter if the person is alive or has passed away.

Remember 1 is the best and 10 is the worst relationship.
3. If you have any questions or concerns about what to do, then simply go back and read over the instructions again. Relax and just let the process do what it is supposed to do.

1. Spouse _____   1a. Ex-Spouse(s) _____, _____
2. Father _____   3. Mother _____
4. Father-in-law _____   5. Mother-in-law _____
6. Brother(s) _____, _____, _____, _____, _____,

7. Sister(s) _____, _____, _____, _____, _____, _____,

8. Adult Son(s) _____, _____, _____, _____, _____,

9. Adult Daughter(s) _____, _____, _____, _____, _____,

10. Teenage Son(s) _____, _____, _____, _____, _____,

11. Teenage Daughter(s) _____, _____, _____, _____,

12. Significant Other _____

13. Men _____   14. Women _____

15. Authority Figures (police, boss, etc.) _____

16. Pastor _____   17. Pastor's Spouse _____

Do not fill in #18 yet. Read the instructions that follow first. Final blank: (Page 157) 18. God _____ (Leave this one blank for now.)

After you have measured each applicable person, then you **MUST** <u>discuss</u> your replies with someone else. It could be in person or over the phone. However you decide to do it, you **MUST** discuss your answers with another person before you complete the <u>final blank.</u> *****<u>While you still have them on the phone or with you,</u> go to the last page of this chapter and fill in the final blank. (pg 157)**

DO NOT TURN THERE UNTIL YOU HAVE FILLED IN AND DISCUSSED ALL OF THE SEVENTEEN BLANKS THAT PERTAIN TO YOU!

Now, after you have filled in blank #18, take time to discuss your results. **<u>After you have discussed your results with a friend, discuss your answers to the following questions.</u>**

1. Were you surprised that your true relationship with God was based on your relationship with other people?
   a. How many times have you read the Epistle of John, and the scriptures quoted in this exercise did not register their true meaning in your heart?
2. Do you understand the importance of having all of your relationships measured as #1?

a. If God has commanded you to love your enemies and to love your neighbor as yourself, then how can you have a relationship that is anything less than #1?

b. Love them because God commanded you to. You cannot let anyone interfere with your relationship with God. It is not about them, but it is about you and God.

3. Who determines the condition of your relationships?

a. Are you basing your relationships on how you think the other person feels about you? If the answer is yes, then it is time that you took charge over the relationships that you have or have been involved in. It does not matter what they say or feel or think about you as far as the relationship is concerned. They have a right to feel, think, and say anything they choose. You cannot control them or their feelings. However, you can control how you feel, think, and what you say about your own relationships.

4. Do you realize that no matter what happened to you in the past, those things are not happening to you right now in the present?

a. The whole point about getting into the present is that is where God lives. He is an ever-present God. If you are forty years old and you are still angry at men, women, parents, ex-friends, etc., for something that happened when you were fifteen, then it is time to get over yourself. Stop letting the fifteen-year-old you of the past run the forty-year-old you of the present. Whatever happened is not happening to you now, so stop using it as an excuse for not forgiving others and disobeying the Word of God.

5. Do you understand that forgiveness can only occur in the present?

a. I have to ask this again to insure that you are crystal clear about forgiveness. If you focus on the incident, then of course you cannot forgive, no matter how long it has been since it happened. (I am not telling you to act as if nothing ever happened. I know some truly horrible things have been done to people of all ages, especially children. Keep your focus on the present. Your healing will take place in the present, not the past. So, if you are ready to be healed, then you must stay in the present.)

The mind presents every thought as if it requires action now. Thoughts are just thoughts. They are not real! They may be about real things, but the actual thought is not real. It can be anything you decide. If you think of a banana, I mean really concentrate on it, can you eat it? No, it is just a thought. No matter how hard you try to change the past, it will not change, no matter how hard you concentrate on it. So leave it alone and move forward into the present. God will heal your heart, but only in the present. Stay in the present and obey God.

6. List five things you have to be "right" about in a relationship.

a. _____
   _____
   _____
   _____
   _____
   _____

b. _____
   _____
   _____
   _____
   _____
   _____

c. _____
_____
_____
_____
_____
_____

d. _____
_____
_____
_____
_____
_____

e. _____
_____
_____
_____
_____
_____

There is a natural tendency in all human beings to be right. However, how you go about being right is the question. Do you make someone wrong to show that you are right? Do you avoid or use the silent treatment until you are acknowledged as being right? Do you get violent, loud, angry, or maybe critical with people until they give in and say you are right? There are many more ways people go about being right. However, there is a price to pay for self-righteousness in your relationships.

7. What does your need to be "right" cost you in relationships?

_____
_____
_____
_____
_____

_____

_____

_____

_____

8. What price do other people have to pay in order to be in a relationship with you?

_____

_____

_____

_____

_____

_____

_____

_____

_____

9. Are you willing to die to self (give up your self-righteousness) in order to have a relationship be successful?
   a. Dying to self is transformation and renewing of the mind. It is referred to in Philippians 2:12, **"work out your own salvation with fear and trembling"**; you must give up those deep-rooted beliefs that have been holding you back and destroying your relationships. Love, joy, and peace will surely fill the void left by the loss of self-righteousness.

10. Can you surrender to the Word of God? It commands you to forgive one another and to love one another now.
    a. **"Let nothing be done through selfish ambition or conceit, but in lowliness of mind let each esteem others better than himself"** (Philippians 2:3).
    b. **"I have been crucified with Christ; it is no longer I who live but Christ lives in me; and the life which I now live in the flesh I live by faith in the Son**

153

of God, who loved me and gave Himself for me" (Galatians 2:20).

c. *"Therefore if you bring your gift to the altar, and there remember that your brother has something against you; leave your gift there before the altar, and go your way. First be reconciled to your brother, and then come and offer your gift"* (Matthew 5:23-24).

God's Word will never change. God will never receive anything from a person with a hard heart (He refused to receive Cain's offering because of his hard and evil heart). You must purpose in your heart, to trust in the Lord, and follow His commands, so that you may receive your reward in loving relationships. Your healing will come in fellowship within the Body of Christ. If you do not want to carry around hurt and pain anymore, surrender it all to the Lord Jesus and be healed. Are you finally ready to leave the past in the past and show up in the present with the Lord, so that you can enter your predestined future?

"Confess your trespasses to one another and pray for one another that you may be healed." (James 5:16)

Consider Your Ways

As you were answering the previous questions after you completed the exercises, did you notice that the only constant person in all of your relationships is you? If you have been involved in ten relationships and you are still looking for the "right" person, I have some good news for you. The person you are looking for does not exist. The "right" person you are looking for only exists in your mind. There are no real people in your mind. So, stop looking there for real relationships.

Instead of looking for the right person for yourself, you have to learn to become the right person for someone else. It is your belief system and your walls that keep people out of your life. Until you change, nothing else can change in your life. That is what transformation is all about. You transform and renew your mind in order to receive from and surrender to the Word of God. God will not transform or renew your mind for you. You must do it yourself. The only way to do it is to be a blessing to someone you're in relationship with.

Have you learned yet that your perfect 10 does not exist? I said I had some good news for you and that's it. Again, you can now stop looking for a dream and start preparing yourself for a real person. Surrender your life to the Lord and He will reveal just who that right person is for your life. And more importantly, the Lord will reveal just who you are and need to be to make that relationship successful.

Jesus makes relationships real. The world has a system of feelings, emotions, thoughts, and dreams on which to base relationships. None of these are credible in a relationship because they are part of self-fulfillment and fleshly desires of the mind. Only your heart/spirit has concern for another person. You can only hear the voice of the Lord in your heart/spirit. Listen for His voice and obey His Word and watch and see all the great blessings He has planned for you through other people in your relationships.

Have you been waiting for a godly relationship in marriage? How long have you been crying out to God? God will not send someone to fulfill your needs because that is not His job. God has heard your request, but first, He wants you to consider your ways.

What Road Are You Traveling On

There is a saying that goes like this, "There is no way to get to where you are going if you don't know where you are." If you call a travel agent to book a trip, what is the most important thing that they need to know? It is not where you're going. It is where you're leaving from. Travel starts from the departure point, not the arrival point. Many people never arrive at their destination because they have no idea where they are leaving from.

There are all kinds of self-help books and mind-over-matter theories in the world. Few if any of them are founded in truth. People are as lost today as ever before. The psychiatric and psychological professions are overcrowded with therapists and the world is crazier than ever. The focus of these theories is the mind. Unfortunately, the answers are not going to be found in the mind, but in the heart. As the heart goes, so goes the entire person. The heart deals with reality not theories. The heart deals with truth not fiction or fantasy.

God's Word in the Bible is truth. It is a foundation from which you can and will know where you are in your life. There is no guesswork or batteries of tests to complete. There are no new theories coming forth each day or new techniques being developed. No, the Word of God is the same yesterday, today, and forever. It will tell you exactly where you are on any given day because the measure that it uses is your personal walk with the Lord.

The Bible says to love <u>God</u> and to love your <u>neighbor</u> as you love <u>yourself</u>. If you do all three, then you will be exactly on course with the Word of God. You will be led by your heart through faith. I know faith cannot be measured, but neither can the thoughts of the minds. However, God is moved by your faith and God moves through faith. What will God do when you operate in faith? All you have to do is read it. The answer is in the Bible. You don't have to guess. Walking by faith (God's way) does not seem natural. Walking by sight (the world's way) does seem natural. Wouldn't you rather freefall with God by faith than walk with the devil?

God requires one thing from His believers and that is to obey His Word. It takes faith and He even provides that for each of you. Apply His Word to whatever situation you are in. Be in right standing with Him, repentant of any sin and watch and see the glory of the Lord show up for you.

God cannot lie. He will keep His Word because His Word is Jesus. You are already in the ultimate relationship. It is with the Lord and Savior, Jesus Christ. He will always be there with you traveling on the road to self-worth.

> *"Trust in the Lord with all your heart*
> *and lean not on your own understanding;*
> *in all your ways acknowledge Him,*
> *and He will direct your paths."*
> *Proverbs 3:5-6*

Praise the Lord!
***

If you have completed all of the instructions from the previous pages on measuring your relationships, you are ready to fill in the final blank. **18. God** _____ (<----- **highest number**).

On the blank next to God, place the <u>HIGHEST</u> number that you placed next to any of the previous relationships that you measured. Again, place the <u>HIGHEST</u> number on the blank next to God. Yes, the highest number is for the worst relationship, not the best.

[10] In this the children of God and the children of the devil are manifest: <u>Whoever does not practice righteousness is not of God, nor is he who does not love his brother.</u>
[11] For this is the message that you heard from the beginning, that <u>we should love one another,</u>
[12] not as Cain who was of the wicked one and murdered his brother. And why did he murder him? Because his works were evil and his brother's righteous.
[13] Do not marvel, my brethren, if the world hates you.
[14] We know that we have passed from death to life, because we love the brethren. <u>He who does not love his brother abides in death.</u>
[15] <u>Whoever hates his brother is a murderer,</u> and you know that no murderer has eternal life abiding in him." I John 3:10-15
[17] Love has been perfected among us in this: that we may have boldness in the day of judgment; because as He is, so are we in this world.
[18] There is no fear in love; but <u>perfect love casts out fear,</u> because fear involves torment. But he who fears has not been made perfect in love.
[19] We love Him because He first loved us.
[20] <u>If someone says, "I love God," and hates his brother, he is a liar; for he who does not love his brother whom he has seen, how can he love God whom he has not seen?</u>
[21] And this commandment we have from Him: that he who loves God must love his brother also." I John 4:17-21

CHAPTER SEVEN
LOVE

LOVE

WHAT IS LOVE
BUT AN OPPORTUNITY
FOR THE HEART TO SING
ITS PRECIOUS MELODY

TO SING LOUD AND CLEAR
WITHOUT KNOWING THE CHORDS
THAT FLOW SO FREELY
FROM A PLACE UNEXPLORED

AS YOU STAND ALL ALONE
IN THE MIDST OF YOUR TEARS
LOVE CONDUCTS THE SYMPHONY
THAT SOOTHES AWAY YOUR FEARS

¹⁶"For God so loved the world that He gave His only begotten Son, that whoever believes in Him should not perish but have everlasting life"
(John 3:16)

The best way of summing up the previous six chapters is to have a better understanding of love. Love is God's best plan for all of mankind. Everything in life comes down to how much you are able to access love. I say "access love" because love is always available to you, but you do not always want it for various reasons. The greatest hindrance to loving someone else is an inability in loving yourself. The love that you receive from God is not yours. It was given to you because God loves you. Once you have it, you can share it with someone else. Do not horde it, because it will not stay where it is not being used. It was given to you to SOW into others, so that they may sow their love into you. You truly reap whatever you sow, therefore, sow God's love.

God's Love and Marriage

In the eyes of God, marriage is not just a legal contract, but a legal covenant. The world's contracts are made to be broken. They have become a game puzzle within the legal system. It's a game to see what lawyer or law firm can come up with the solution to get around the signed contract. It is not that way with God. Whatever you speak as a vow is recorded in the annals of heaven for all time. You will see it again on the Day of Judgment. It doesn't matter what laws are passed or what rulings courts or judges make concerning marriage, because God has already spoken on the subject. They can say a marriage is between a person and a fish (I hope no one gets any ideas from this) and pass all of the laws they wish to support it, but it will not stand with the Lord. In the beginning, they were Adam and Eve, not Adam and Ed or Aida and Eve. Marriage is between a man and a woman, period.

Psalms 12:8 says, ***"The wicked prowl on every side, when <u>vileness is exalted</u> among the sons (and daughters) of men."*** God says that <u>homosexuality</u> is an <u>abomination</u> in His eyes. The vileness of a sexual relationship between people of the same sex is exalted today in many countries. It has even been excused away as a human gene that some people just happen to have. However, God says that He created them male and female. Choose who you will believe, God or scientists. Who is lying? I want you to know that it is not a matter of scientific research, but a matter of satanic intervention that came up with that absurd theory. When people blatantly lie and obscure facts in order to validate their own theories, then satanic intervention is definitely involved. John 8:44 says, ***"for he (Satan) is a liar and the father of it."*** Is homosexuality caused by some aberrant gene or is it a choice of sexual behavior? If you believe it is caused by some aberrant gene, then what gene causes heterosexuality? Genes do not cause gender, they are a part of a person's predetermined gender. God determines the gender.

I had to bring back the topic of homosexuality in this chapter because of marriage and because of love. People talk about love and loving as if it is a feeling that comes and goes as **it** pleases. Basing a marriage on love for each other is great, if and only if that love lines up with the Word of God. Love seems to be the justifier for practically anything and everything people do these days. Can you murder someone and justify it by saying it was because you truly loved them? What kind of love is that?

Is it love that justifies the murder of babies because they interfere with your sex life, lifestyle, dating life, dress size, mental state, professional life, present relationship, future relationships, cash flow, or because neither of you are ready to raise children? Is it love that justifies divorcing the one you use to love because you have met someone else that you now love? Since all these things are done in the name of love, did God tell you to do them? Some people even say God told them to divorce their spouse and marry someone else. What God are they talking about?

Additionally, can you love someone so much that you just cannot live without them? (How did you live long enough to meet them in the first place?) So, now that they are gone are you suicidal? What kind of love is this? Can you abuse your spouse or even murder him or her because you love them so much? Can you abuse your children or even murder them because you love them so much? Can you love God so much that you hate other people because of their skin color, nationality, sexual choices, or religious preferences? Did God make a big mistake because He did not make them just like you? When you speak of love in terms of your sex life, your emotions, and how you feeeeel about someone is that really love too? Wow, isn't love just wonderful!

The Bible tells us to love one another. It also tells husbands to love their wives. So which one of the loves listed in the paragraphs above, or any other love that you can think of do you use for marriage? God commands us to love one another. So, what love is God talking about? Is God's love for mankind the same as mankind's love for Him? In the Book of Romans 5:5, it says, ***"Now hope does not disappoint, because the <u>love of God</u> has been poured out in our <u>hearts</u> by the <u>Holy Spirit</u> who was given to us."*** The "love of God" is the love that He gives to us for marriage and relationships. It comes to us by the Holy Spirit. Do you know the Holy Spirit? Do you spend time talking with the Holy Spirit? Do you believe there is a Holy Spirit? If not, then how did you access the love of God?

If you are married or desire to be married, you need to understand what the love of God is, and not the world's interpretation of love. Love cannot be hurtful and comforting; caring and loathing; kind and hateful; good and evil. Love is not about how you feeeeeel and love is not sex or your lustful desire for someone. What does love mean to you? What kind of love are you choosing to use to love someone else? If it is all about your feeeeeelings, emotions, and uncontrollable desires, then it is lust and there is no love in it. God's love is from the heart and there is no fear in it. God's love is described as follows:

> *4* *"**Love** suffers long and is kind; **love** does not envy;*
> *   **love** does not parade itself, is not puffed up;*
> *   5 does not behave rudely, does not seek its own,*
> *   is not provoked, thinks no evil;*
> * 6 does not rejoice in iniquity, but rejoices in the truth;*
> *   7 bears all things, believes all things, hopes*
> *   all things, endures all things.*
> *   8 "**Love** never fails..."*
> * 11 "When I was a child, I spoke as a child, I understood*
> *   as a child, I thought as a child; but when I*
> *   became a man, I put away childish things.*
> * 12 For now we see in a mirror, dimly, but then face to*
> *   face. Now I know in part, but then I shall*
> *   know just as I also am known.*
> *   13 And now abide faith, hope, **love**, these three;*
> *   but the greatest of these is **love**."*
> *   I Corinthians 13:4-6, 8, 11-13*

I have had many Christians tell me that they no longer love their spouse or they will say that they have fallen out of love with their spouse. I had to wonder just how can that happen; how is that possible? If the love of God comes from God and it is poured into our hearts by the Holy Spirit, then something must have happened to the source of their love. I know people think that love is theirs and they

164

can give it to anyone they choose or take it away from anyone they choose, but that is not true. If you no longer love someone, then the source of your love is no longer in place. You cannot give your love away any longer because you don't have it to give. Your problem is not with your spouse or with another person. Your problem is with God who is love's source. I John 4:7-8 says, *"Beloved, let us love one another for love is of God; and everyone who loves is born of God and knows God. He who does not love does not know God, for God is love."*

The real breakdown is not in your relationship with your spouse, but in your relationship with God. If you would turn to God and "ask" Him to restore your relationship with Him, He would. Of course, there may be a need for repentance or forgiveness, but God will always be there when you call. I have seen marriages turned around in a day after years of fighting and abuse. All it takes is a sincere heart, repentance, forgiveness, and a willingness to apply the Word of God. God can and He will restore the flow of love into your marriage or relationship. Remember, it is the love of God, not the love you make up that will turn things around. I Corinthians 13:8 says, *"Love never fails."* I Peter 4:8 says, *"And above all things have fervent love for one another, for love will cover a multitude of sins."*

Your marriage is much too important to bring a counterfeit version of love into the relationship. Satan is the great counterfeiter. Have you been duped into using one of his counterfeit versions of God's love? You don't have to guess about this. You already know if the love you say you have for your spouse is real or not. All you have to do is look at the results of your marriage to date. Is it growing and getting better and better? Is it a struggle and time sensitive because you don't know how much longer you will be married? It's up to you to throw out the counterfeit and replace it with the true love of God. God's love is always available to you. If you want it, all you have to do is ask.

God Is Love!

Let's be perfectly clear about the fact that God is Love. There is no love source anywhere in the world. All love must come from God. Romans 5:5 says, *"Now hope does not disappoint, because the love of God has been poured out in our hearts by the Holy Spirit who was given to us."* Unless love has been poured into *your* heart by the Holy Spirit, you do not have love. If you do not know Jesus, the Son of God, then you do not have love.

The love that the Father pours out into your heart is only for those who know Jesus as their Lord and Savior. John 14:6-7 says, *⁶"Jesus said to him, I am the way, the truth, and the life. No one comes to the Father except through Me. ⁷If you had known Me, you would have known My Father also; and from now on you know Him and have seen Him."* If you know Jesus, then love is available to you.

> ⁷ *"Beloved, let us love one another, for love is of God;*
> *and everyone who loves is born of God and knows God.*
> ⁸ *He who does not love does not know God, for <u>God is love</u>.*
> ⁹ *In this the love of God was manifested toward us, that God*
> *has sent His only begotten Son into the world, that we might live*
> *through Him.*
> ¹⁰ *In this is love, not that we loved God, but that*
> *He loved us and sent His Son to be the propitiation for our sins.*
> ¹¹ *Beloved, if God so loved us, we also ought to love one*
> *another."*
> *I John 4:7-11*

Now, you may think you have love, but is it only lust? Yes, lust, the love of the flesh, the love of the mind. Lust of the flesh will always lead to sin if you do not take authority over it quickly. This is the worldly love that disappears after three years or after seven years as the world teaches. You know the seven-year itch and all of the other nonsense. God's love does not get weaker, but it gets stronger each and every day as you pursue Him. God is the ONLY source of love.

166

If you are not "born-again," then it is impossible to have the love of God. Of course you will have all of the feeeeelings and emotions of the flesh, but that is as far as it will ever go. How often do you hear people say, how they were so much in love with each other? Then how could it have ended? Whatever your flesh desires today, it will desire something different tomorrow and the next day and so on and so on. The desires of the flesh are like an all-consuming fire that never gets enough. Do what the Word of God says to do, take authority over your flesh.

Why is it that people have such a hard time loving God, their neighbors, and themselves? Is it because of a lack of knowledge about love or because you are being deceived? If it is a lack of knowledge, then read God's Word daily (memorize I Corinthians chapter 13). If it is because you are being deceived, then you need to know, once again the devil has a counterfeit plan for God's love and that plan is called lust. Lust is based in <u>fear</u>. It has something to do with the fact that love and fear cannot exist within you at the same time. <u>The counterfeit of love is lust</u>. Love always has the power to overcome fear.

Fear is <u>f</u>alse <u>e</u>vidence <u>a</u>ppearing <u>r</u>eal. It is false evidence because the enemy has a counterfeit version of everything. Fear justifies <u>not</u> loving someone else, as well as not loving yourself. Fear is an excuse for not showing up in the present and a reason for continuing to hold onto the past. Fear is a choice, a decision not to have faith in God's gift of love. <u>Fear is a blindfold over your heart and a window for the mind to pursue its lust of the flesh</u>. Do not let fear blind you to the love that exists in those who love you. Love is not in your mind, it is only in your heart. Don't try to figure it all out. You just have to freefall with love and trust that God will always be there to catch you.

LOVE & FEAR

Within your life
There exists a pair
One is love
The other is fear
\/

From an early age
You knew which one
Fulfilled all your dreams
From the other you run
\/

You quickly became a
Confirmed doubting Thomas
From your first disappointment
To your last broken promise
\/

Sides were taken
In love you felt used
Fear seemed a safe place
To conceal all your blues
\/

So many like you
With stories to tell
Of hearts that were broken
And affairs that failed

As victims you're smothered
With sympathy and support
Weakened each time
By the tales you report
\/

Your power and strength
Lay there by your feet
Completely unnoticed
Beneath your defeats
\/

Life is a roller coaster
Filled with ups and downs
But you don't have to ride it
'Til it slams to the ground
\/

When your tears stop falling
And your spine straightens out
You'll begin to recognize
What your life's all about
\/

Love is your power
Vulnerable, though it seems
There is strength in compassion
Joy again in your dreams

Love is the answer
Give it freely to all
Life rises in love
In fear life falls

Love and fear are in a tug-of-war in your life; which one will win? If you allow it, love will conquer all. Love will not leave you or forsake you. It will always be right there, where you left it before fear showed up in your life. Speak to fear and command it to GO in the name of Jesus and watch it flee in terror from your presence.

I certainly hope that love reigns in your life on a daily basis; if not, I think I might have some words of encouragement for you. You do not have to earn love from anyone. As a matter of fact, you cannot earn love. Love is unconditional. I was going to say true love is unconditional, but there are no <u>degrees</u> of love. I know people say that there are degrees of love, tough love for example. If there is tough love, then there must also be weak love. So then if there are degrees of love, who do you give these different types of love to? Do they earn them or do they deserve or not deserve them? Do they even have the right to accept or not accept these types of love? There aren't different types of love, only a lack of knowledge and understanding of love.

I don't believe there are various types or amounts of love. You either love someone or you do not. Anything else is a cover-up for a lack of loving unconditionally, but more realistically, it is a cover-up for not knowing how to love someone else. You see, deep down inside, people think and believe that their love has to be earned or has to be deserved. Why not! They had to earn all the love they have received thus far in life. So why shouldn't everyone else earn love the way they had to?

While we may not consciously have this conversation, it definitely shows up this way in our relationships. Your ability to love someone else sets the foundation for building your relationships. Relationships help to define your ability to love. The quality of your relationships is your feedback on how well you are doing.

This may come as a shock to people who have learned about love from movies, soaps, and dopes, but love does not curse you out or slap you around; it does not threaten to leave you, harm you, or kill you; and it does not belittle you; it does not stress you out; it does not condemn you and it does not take or steal all your money. Love does not try to make you responsible for the mess that others have made of their own lives; and it does not place parents, siblings, former friends, work, or the **call into ministry** before you. Love never fails. However, the devil's counterfeit of love, which is lust, always fails. All of the things that I added after the scriptures are based in a relationship built on lust. These things (behaviors) are never found in God's love.

To better understand love, let's talk about lust and the source of lust. Lust is fear-based and attached to the sin of pride. The lust of the mind/flesh is the counterfeit model Satan uses to oppose the love of the spirit/heart. Lust always involves the desires of the five senses. God created the five senses for good. They are the direct channel or link from the outside world into your minds. They are the "feelers" of the mind. Their importance to your daily life is enormous. However, try to remember that the five senses only provide information to your mind that still must be evaluated and translated into useful and purposeful knowledge. This information does not have to be understood to be implemented into action by the mind; it just must be received. Also keep in mind that this information feed is mixed with emotions and past experiences. That's why the saying "seeing is believing" is NOT a true statement.

Is Seeing Believing

If seeing is not believing, then the opposite must be true, believing is seeing. As a matter of fact we see hundreds even thousands of things daily that we do not believe because they do not register in our minds until they become beliefs. Show a picture to five different people and then ask them what they saw and you will get five different answers. However, let them study the picture for a while and then ask them what they saw and the answers will begin to match. The images in the picture will begin to register in their minds as they spend time studying them.

On one of the next few pages, I have written a short verse. Take no more than <u>five seconds</u> to read this verse, then turn immediately to the next page and follow the directions. Remember, take no more than **five seconds** to look at the verse and turn immediately to the next page.

Keep your word!

Five seconds only

Ready!

Turn the page

————————————————————

————————————————————

————————————————————

————————————————————

| A   PARIS |

| |

| BIRD   IN THE |

| IN THE   AND   THE |

| THE   SPRING |

| HAND   TIME |

————————————————————

————————————————————

————————————————————

————————————————————

Did you keep your word and take only five seconds? Great! So, what did you read? Was it?

A BIRD IN THE HAND   yes _____ no _____
(check one)

PARIS IN THE SPRING TIME   yes _____ no _____
(check one)

Now go back and look again and see what's really there.

If you had heard of or knew these verses beforehand, then your mind would automatically see what you already knew to be true. The mind sees only what it already believes. If a pink elephant suddenly appeared in front of you in your home, you would not believe it because you already know there is no such thing as a pink elephant. Moreover, you know that elephants do not appear, suddenly or otherwise, especially in your home. You wouldn't tell anyone, because they would think you had truly lost it. So, the mind would simply dismiss the appearance and begin to convince you it did not happen.

However, if you began to hear about pink elephants suddenly appearing in front of people in their homes, then you would begin to rethink what you saw and more than likely jump on the bandwagon and let people know you were also one of the privileged ones. Next you would join a special club of other privileged ones who have seen the once unheard of pink elephant. You would all create chat rooms, Web sites, and e-mail addresses for this exclusive club and so on. The excitement would grow and next thing you would all be talking about seeing flying saucers and little green spacemen. **The mind is a terrible thing to waste!**

It is a struggle to get the mind to see anything differently than what is already programmed into it. It does not happen by accident. It happens by choice. As I have stated before we are our beliefs and we absolutely choose the beliefs we have become. Once a belief is formed, it takes a concerted conscious effort to change or remove the belief. This process is called Transformation and Renewing the Mind.

Jesus talked about how difficult it is to change your old beliefs in Luke 5:37-38. He described it as trying to pour new wine into old wineskins because the new wine will burst the old wineskin. The old wineskin will resist change as if change was not possible. The mind resists change and therefore, you must transform it in order to grow and add new things to what you already know. The mind transforms with changes in the heart. It takes the Word of God to change the heart. The Word of God will drive all unrighteousness from your heart.

But It's How I Feel

Getting back to the five senses, you must recognize that the information furnished by the five senses is not automatically believed because it must fit into your belief system before you can fully accept it. Once this information has become a part of your belief system, then subsequent similar information is automatically believed. Please do not underestimate the power of the five senses. They are the receptors of the flesh and mind. Therefore, how you feel about a subject can outweigh what you know about that same subject. When this happens, you have entered into a very dangerous place in your life. Truth no longer has the power to influence your life (a desire to know) and feelings and emotions now control your life.

Have you heard people say, "if it feels good, do it"? When feelings take over, reality no longer matters and ceases to exist for you. Soon you become an old wineskin and the only thing that matters is the past, what you already know and understand. Change becomes almost impossible for you. You have just given the enemy permission to attack you with depression, anxiety, breakdowns, etc. How you feel has become a wall and reality just bounces off of it. You are now stuck with all of your previous beliefs with no hope of changing any of them, even if your life is at stake.

Here is where you come back to love's counterfeit once again. Lust is only about the past. Since it is rooted in fear and pride, lust will seek out exactly what it wants because you deserve it. Sins of the flesh are committed because you believe you deserve to have the desires of your flesh. No one person or thing is more important than your desire to fulfill what you believe you deserve. Your eyes may desire to see nudity, sex acts, and all kinds of sexual perversion. It will not matter if you are married and have children who will be hurt by this desire; your desire will win out. Even if you have to go through a divorce to have your fleshly desires fulfilled, you will do it. You may even blame your spouse for your problem. Listen, your spouse cannot compete with your desire for pornography. Your spouse is no match for the sins your mind can conceive concerning your sexual desires.

Don't be surprised if you blame your spouse for your failure to take authority over your perverted thoughts. You will actually believe that if she really loved you, she should willingly do anything and everything your mind conceives, to make you happy. Since she refuses, it has to be her fault for your failure. She must be responsible for your fleshly desires because if she would just "obey" you everything would be okay. NOT!

Lustful desires will only lead to more lustful desires, like another all consuming fire. Lust is of the devil, so why would you want it in your marriage? Perversion is of the devil, so who is your lord? God gave you a wife to be a helpmate in worshipping Him, not for serving the devil. Listen to your wife and stand together and put 10,000 demonic attacks, against you and your marriage, to flight.

The reality of the spirit of lust is that it has come for your very life. It is all spiritual warfare. The demonic forces have come only *"to steal, kill and to destroy"* (John 10:10). Lust has come to steal your joy, spouse, and family. It has come to destroy your relationships with the opposite sex, including your sons and daughters. Lust loathes the opposite sex and has a total disrespect for them. However, you cannot disrespect anyone more than you disrespect yourself. Lust has come to kill you, your spouse, and if you allow it, your children too. It will use violence, depression, and even the spirit of suicide to attack you and your family. Just remember, you gave it permission and you must continue to give it permission in order for it to keep on consuming your life. No spirit of evil has any authority over you. It must have your permission to steal, kill, or destroy you.

If it feels good, do it. It is the mantra of the Baby Boomer generation. How many lives will continue to be destroyed by this belief? People are even being taught to base their marriages and relationships on how they feeeeeel. They seek counsel that confirms their feelings not counsel that confirms the truth. (Homosexuality, pedophilia, and other perversions are based on feeeeeelings. If they feel like it, it must be okay, so do it.) In I Corinthians Chapter 13, there is not one reference between love and how you feel. There is no mention of feeeeeelings or emotions. Love has nothing to do with how you feeeeeel. Nothing whatsoever!

Have you ever heard people say, "I do not think I love you anymore because I do not feeeeeel the same way I did when I met you"? "I do not love you any more because you do not turn me on like you use to do when we first met"? "I have fallen out of love with you because I do not feeeeeel the same way about you"? "I do not love you anymore because you have changed, and my feeeeeelings have changed toward you"? I know that people think that they are sincere when they say these things, but they do not realize that what they are saying is not founded on truth or anywhere in the Word of God.

First of all, you are NOT your feelings! Feelings are something you have, they are not something that you are. I'm including emotions in this also. Whatever you believed about being loved or not being loved, you brought into your relationship. When confronted with a genuine request to give of yourself in love, you check your feelings and not your heart. You check your mind and not your heart. The truth is, you cannot give love because you do not know how. Who taught you how to give love? Who taught you how to love unconditionally? The answer for most people is no one. No one has taught you because the source of love is not your spouse or parents or friends; again, the source of love is God (I John 4:7-8); *"Beloved, let us love one another, for love is of God; and everyone who loves is born of God and knows God. He who does not love does not know God, for God is love."*

When you begin to say you do not love someone anymore, what you are really saying is you have broken your relationship with God and therefore, your source for love is no longer available to you. Again, in the Book of Romans 5:5 it says**, *"Now hope does not disappoint, because the love of God has been poured out in our hearts by the Holy Spirit who was given to us."* God pours out His love, through the Holy Spirit, into your heart, not your mind, not your flesh, not your feelings, but into your heart. Is your heart hard and cold toward someone else? Then love is not available to you. You have cut yourself off the source of love by the hardness of your heart. Divorce comes because of the hardness of your heart. A hard heart causes broken relationships with people as well as with God. But the relationship is broken with God first.

As I said in the marriage chapter, the vow in marriage is to your spouse first and to God second. (You must speak your vow to a person in marriage first before God honors it.) <u>It is the vertical relationship with God that must be set aside before the horizontal relationship with a person can be destroyed in divorce.</u> God warned you in Ecclesiastes 5:4, do not vow to God and then break it (paraphrased). What filthy demonic spirits are you associating with that have convinced you to break your relationship with God? It is not your spouse that you no longer love, it's God!

I know the things I am saying are hard to receive, but I did not write them, I am simply pointing them out. God commanded us to do three things and said that on these three things "hang all the Law and the Prophets" (Matthew 22:37-38): ***You shall <u>love the Lord your God</u> with all your heart, with all your soul, and with all your mind. This is the first and great commandment. And the second is like it: You shall <u>love</u> your <u>neighbor</u> as <u>yourself</u>.***"

Love God, your neighbor, and yourself, these are the three. There will never be a neighbor or brother closer to you than your spouse (a vowed relationship to God). Then how can anyone say they love God and hate their spouse? In I John 4:20, it says, ***"If someone says, I love God, and hates his brother, he is a <u>liar</u>."*** Do not be a liar. Trust in God, He is love.

Love is from God and the spirit of lust is from the devil. In the world people talk often about how much they love each other. If they do not know Jesus as their Lord and Savior, then how can they possibly love each other? Jesus is God! If you do not know Jesus, then where are you going to get access to His great gift of love? The only thing the world has access to is the counterfeit spirit of lust.

The worldly speak in terms of "I want you; I need you; I cannot live without you; you are my destiny; my life is nothing without you," etc. All those terms that they say to other people should actually be spoken to God. How can another person be the fulfillment of your life? What a burden to place on someone else, trying to make them responsible for your life. Think of how selfish and sorry you have to be to hold someone else accountable for your happiness or for your life. Responsibility can never be delegated to anyone, especially the responsibility for your own life.

Everyone will be held accountable for everything that they do and say. There will be a written account of it on Judgment Day. Being accountable for something is not the same as being responsible for it. The confusion comes when someone wants to hold someone else accountable for their mistakes. Since they never make mistakes, it must be someone else's fault. If you feel you need to make an excuse for what you did, then that is a good indicator that you are both responsible and accountable. Did you notice that you are also missing character, integrity, and honor? No wonder you find it hard to love yourself, your neighbor, and God. The world's system has a way of making others responsible, accountable, at fault, and to blame for your mistakes as well as your sins. It will never be that way with God.

No wonder the majority of murders are among family members. The worldly say blood is thicker than water. They also say, you only hurt the ones you love." How absurd! No, you hurt the ones you lust for, or you lust for the things they have. There is no hurt in love. You don't love the ones you hurt. You don't love anyone, and that's the problem.

Who really is the lord of your life? It certainly is not the Lord Jesus. Are you a child of the devil, carrying out his plan to steal, kill, and destroy? Are you willing to start loving with your heart and not with your head/mind? If so, repent and just do it God's way. Stop making excuses. Remember, people know you by what you say, but they define you by what you do. How do people defined you?

Love Never Fails

Love never fails. First, you must find the source to that love in your heart. Each person has to make that decision for his or her own life. How many failed relationships do you have to have before you get it? God is the source. It has been this way from the beginning and that is just the way it is, even today. Jesus is the answer. He is the door into the real world you are searching for. Stop repeating your mistakes and just surrender to the Lord. His Word is true and it is truth. Let God bless you with His love. Proverbs 10:22 says, *"The blessing of the Lord makes one rich, and He adds no sorrow with it."*

The world is seeking happiness and they cannot find it. Happiness does not exist by itself. Happiness is a result of **JOY**. There is no happiness apart from joy, and joy is the fruit of the Holy Spirit. Searching for happiness will take you to all the wrong places and bring all the wrong people into your life. It does not exist by itself, so stop looking for it where it does not exist. The answers are all written down in the Bible, so that no one can say they did not know where to find them, on the Day of Judgment.

The fruit of the Spirit is:

"love, joy, peace, longsuffering, kindness, goodness, faithfulness, gentleness, self-control"
(Galatians 5:22-23)

Are you searching for any of this fruit for your life? If so, go to the source. If you are born-again all of the fruit is already in your heart. You do not have to ask for it, you just have to access it. If you are not born-again you need to know that you will not find it in a bottle, in a needle, in a whorehouse, in a cult, or in any form of sin. If you've been searching all of your life, don't give up. You will have to come to the source and the source is the Holy Spirit. He will love you unconditionally.

Remember, searching for love is fruitless. Go to the source. It does not exist outside of God the Father, God the Son, and God the Holy Spirit. God is waiting on you. He will not stop loving you, so you may as well jump on board and start loving Him back. Love God with all your heart, soul, and mind; and love yourself. Stay in hot pursuit of the Lord. You cannot out love God, but it is sure a lot of fun trying.

Take your eyes off of your problems or the situation that is confronting you in the moment. God knows it's there and He already has a plan to remove your situation so that you will have a testimony of His glory. Look around and see who needs your assistance and who needs your unconditional love. Know in your heart that God put them there to partner with you and help you mature in His love. Release His love through your compassion for others.

Relationships are the key. Everything God has planned for you is connected to your relationship with Him. His assignment for you is to tell someone about Jesus. God has hand picked you to reach the lost. He has saved you specifically for this season in creation. Just stay focused on the prize.

God is looking for Disciples to carry His Gospel to the entire world. I know that millions of people will never read His Word in the Bible. That is why God is always looking for faithful people who will obey Him and have compassion in their hearts for the lost. There is still much work to be done in the world to spread the Gospel. Focus on what God has called you to do as an individual. Check your heart to see who it is you have compassion for. God put that compassion on your heart on purpose and it will reveal your assignment.

Compassion is a burning desire to act when a need arises and not to just be an observing sympathizer. Sympathy is feeling with no healing. Jesus was never sympathetic, but He was compassionate (feeling with healing). Compassion is driven by your love for God. Your love for your neighbor is a reflection of the love you have for yourself. Loving yourself is the key. Loving yourself is what the fuss is all about. You can say you love God and you can say that you love yourself, but if you do not love your neighbor, you are far from God. Your neighbor is the common denominator between you and the Father. Your love for you neighbor is evidence of your love for God and yourself.

On a scale of 1 – 10, 1 being the best and 10 being the worst of relationships, what measure do you give to yourself? Are you a 1 yet? If not what still stands in your way? Is it fear? Take authority over it in the name of Jesus. From this moment on, fear has no authority in your life because you are a child of love. Life rises in love and in fear it falls. Let love heal you, guide you, and lead you on the road to self-worth.

Love conquers all!

Praise the Lord!
***

***

Love in your heart
Wasn't put there
To stay
Love isn't love
'Til you give
It away

***

CONCLUSION

I wrote this book for the following reasons:

1. To give all glory to God
2. To bring the Word of salvation to the lost
3. To edify the Body of Christ.
4. To heal marriages
    a. Put an end to the horrific problem of divorce within the Body of Christ
5. To restore families
6. To train disciples—church leaders
7. To bring clarity and personal awareness to the Body of Christ in their relationship with the Father.

I believe that all the above purposes are necessary today. There are too many defeated Christians within the Body of Christ because they lack knowledge and common sense concerning the Word of God. I hope that I have stirred up some sense of strength and boldness within the hearts of my brothers and sisters in Christ. The time to turn from being attacked to being the attacker is here. Christians should be armed and dangerous (**spiritually**) at all times.

The Body of Christ is built on the family unit. Marriage is sacred in the eyes of God. It does not matter what laws or statutes the world comes up with that are contrary to the Word of God. God's Word will never change, for anyone. Ensure that your marriage is in order, in God's order. Follow God's rules, laws, and commandments for marriage and you <u>must</u> have a successful marriage.

Husbands, love your wives is the key to all Christian marriages, because without the love of the "head of the household," defeat is certain within that family. Wives, submit to your husbands because you are commanded to do so. I know that the latest women's liberation platform is against it, but if it is not of God, then it is of the devil. You decide what is right, but base it on the Word of God. The family is the husband and the wife and God adds children to that family. God loves family. He has one and it gets bigger and bigger every day as another person accepts His Son, Jesus, as their Lord and Savior.

God hates divorce (Malachi 2:16). It is not just a reference to His people Israel, but to his creation, mankind. If you vow to God (to each other first, then God honors it), then keep it, for life. You will not stay married following the world's system of always taking for yourself and always placing yourself first in the marriage. Marriage is give and give, not give and take. What do you bring to the marriage or to the relationship? If you are looking for someone to make your life better, then His name is Jesus, not your spouse. Trust in God and do it His way. He has the answers you are looking for. **The answer is Jesus!**

> *34* *"A new commandment I give to you, that you love one another; as I have loved you, that you also love one another.*
> *35* *By this all will know that you are My disciples, if you have love for one another."*
> *John 13:34-35*

The most powerful weapon that God has given to all of mankind to use against the deceptions of the enemy is love. Love is God's Master Plan. There is no law, strength, power, or evil device that can stand against love. From the beginning of God's creation to the final Day of Judgment, God's love conquered all. *Love* or some form of the word *love* is used over 500 times in the Bible. I think that God is attempting to make His point. Because God is love! Love drives away all fear. Love heals all wounds and hurts. Love conquers all!

Jesus said in II Corinthians 10:3-6,

> *"For though we walk in the flesh, we do not war according to the flesh. ⁴For the weapons of our warfare are not carnal but mighty in God for pulling down strongholds, ⁵casting down arguments [vain imaginations] and every high thing that exalts itself against the knowledge of God, bring every thought into captivity to the obedience of Christ, ⁶and being ready to punish all disobedience when your obedience is fulfilled."*

God did not create mankind to lose or to be a loser. Mankind's struggles today are no different than those of 6,000 years ago. The struggles are still choosing God over evil. The results of mankind's struggles are the same as before too, *"the wages of sin is death"* (Romans 6:23). Even with the Word of God written down, for 2,000 years as the New Covenant or Testament, the struggles and problems that mankind faces appear to be getting worse. I said *appear* because in actuality, Christianity is growing faster than ever before throughout the world. Churches are increasing in size into the hundreds of thousands of members. Soon, the proliferation of evil will come to an end and the reign of our Lord and Savior, Jesus Christ will begin. Soon the end will come, but not before the work of this generation is completed.

The Gospel of Jesus Christ will be preached throughout all the world. The end of the reign of terror by the devil is also within sight. Jesus said that He came to *"destroy the works of the devil"* (I John 3:8). Do you think that Jesus was able to accomplish that? Or do you think that He failed? Of course Jesus accomplished all that He came on this Earth to do. The problem is that the many people in the Body of Christ who say that they are "believers" do not know this or understand this as fact. The devil is defeated! He is not going to be defeated on Judgment Day; no, he is already defeated.

Again, *"The Road to Self Worth"* is written for Disciples and believers. It is time to walk in the authority of the Lord Jesus. It is time to walk in divine health, be out of debt, and be equipped to tell someone about the Lord Jesus. I pray that all of these things and more are bestowed on your life. Prepare to receive great and wonderful gifts from your Father in heaven. Pursue His righteousness and He will use you "to make a difference in the lives of the people that you are with, so that we can all make a difference in the world."

Praise the Lord!

***

PRAYER OF SALVATION

Of course, if you have not received Jesus as your Lord and Savior, then that is the first step. Give your life over to the Lord Jesus. Open up your heart to receive all the promises of God and all the blessings of God. Receive your salvation and a place with the Lord Jesus for all eternity. Just read the following passage and confess out loud the prayer that follows:

"If you confess with you mouth the Lord Jesus and believe in your heart that God has raised Him from the dead, you will be saved. [10]For with the heart one believes unto righteousness, and with the mouth confession is made unto salvation."

(Romans 10:9-10)

Prayer of salvation: (pray out loud)
Father God, I come before you in the name of Jesus.
I believe in my heart that Jesus died for my sins.
I believe You raised Jesus from the dead and He is alive and in heaven. I confess that Jesus is now my Lord and Savior. I repent of all my sin. I renounce Satan and all his evil works. I believe that I am saved and one day I will be with You in heaven for all eternity. I believe that I am now a born-again follower of Jesus Christ.

I praise you Lord!

Amen

If you prayed this prayer, you are now born-again. All your sins are forgiven, every sin from the first time you (knowingly) sinned until this moment. You are now a Christian.

Praise the Lord!

- If you do not have a Bible, get one and read it
daily. Start with the New Testament and read
as much as you can daily.
- If you do not belong to a Christian church,
then find one in your area, or e-mail me and
I will help you locate a believing church.
- God has great things ahead for you, so get
into fellowship with other believers and disciples
who can help you, teach you, and edify you.

Congratulations!

Welcome to the Body of Christ.

***

ACKNOWLEDGEMENTS

Leo J. Bogee III, my son, who would not let me rest until I completed this book (yes, I'm already working on Parts II & III)

Dr. Dick Chadwick, for years of friendship, support, and encouragement

David Day, my attorney, friend and advisor, for believing in me, I would not be this far without all of your support—thanks also to Rhonda

Billy Duhay, my friend through thick and thin, business associate, confidant and constant encourager, a true family man of God

Pastors Steve and Tina Gunn, for your encouragement and training in the marriage ministry

Irene Ilalio, for your awesome book cover and graphic art designs

Don James, my close friend, for web design and hosting, thank for all of your support and encouragement for my ministry—thanks also to Margie

Pastors David and Debbie Katina, my pastors, for your invaluable encouragement and support in ministry, for giving my family a church home in our time of need and for your love and compassion for your church family

Martha Khlopin, financial advisor, counselor, motivator, friend, for your vision and insight into my life, for speeding up the process of success for my family

Pastor Victor Kila, for your friendship, faith and trust in my ministry

Bishop L.T. Mason, for your faith and trust in my ministry

Pastors Kevin and Lauwae MacKenzie, for your unconditional love and support for me and my family

James and Nellie Menifee, editing and content, flow of ideas, two of my oldest, dearest, and closest friends, thanks for all your hard work

Pastors Richard and Bernice Prasad, for your friendship and trust

Pastor Kennedy Siaosi, for your friendship, faith and trust in my ministry

Pastor Yvonne Soliz, for your friendship, faith and trust in my ministry

Pastor Wayne Speer, for leading me to the Lord, God bless you

Bob and Kandie Stevens, close friends and confidant, partners in ministry, you are always there for support and encouragement, you are a blessing

Pastor Debra Thompson, for your faith and trust in my ministry

Bishop Soala Tupua, friend and encourager, for focus and clarity, faith and trust in my ministry, I greatly appreciate you and Annette

Pastors Mark and Pamela Thompson, you are one of the finest example of godly parents, family leadership, and compassion for people in the Body of Christ. I thank God for your friendship and support for my family & ministry.

Also, there are many ministers of God who had an indirect yet transforming impact on my life in ministry and on this project, these are just a few:

Dr John Avanzini—Pastor Mike Barber—Pastor Tommy Barnett—Pastor J.R. Bernard—Bishop Charles Blake—Bishop Keith Butler—Rev Charles Capps—Pastor Caesar Castellanos—Dr David Jonggi Cho—Dr Edwin Louis Cole—Pastor Bayless Conley—Rev Kenneth & Gloria Copeland—Pastor Wayne Cordeiro—Peter J. Daniels—Dr Charles Dobson—Dr Creflo Dollar—Rev Jesse Duplantis—Pastor Tony Evans—Rev Billy Graham—Dr Franklin Graham—Pastor John Hagee—Pastor Marilyn Hickey—Pastor Benny Hinn—Pastor

Larry Huch—Bishop T.D. Jakes—Bishop Eddie Long—Pastor Keith Moore—Pastors Randy & Roberta Morrison—Pastor Myles Munroe—Dr Mike Murdock—Rev Mario Murillo—Dr Joyce Meyer—Pastor Rod Parsley—Bishop G.E. Patterson—Dr Frederick K.C. Price—Pastor Wayne Speer—Pastors Art & Kuna Sepulveda—Pastor Larry Stockstill—Bishop Perry Stone—Dr Lester Sumrall—Dr Leroy Thompson—Pastors Casey & Wendy Treat—Pastors Randy & Paula White—Pastor Bill Winston

The Ministers that I have listed above have impacted their cities, states, and the world for Jesus Christ. Their anointed teachings are available to anyone who desires to be blessed through by their books, tapes, and CD's, Websites, and television ministries.

Printed in the United States
116988LV00002B/226-309/A